HISTORY

OF

No. 30 SQUADRON

EGYPT AND MESOPOTAMIA

1914 TO 1919

The Naval & Military Press Ltd

Published by
The Naval & Military Press Ltd
5 Riverside, Brambleside, Bellbrook
Industrial Estate, Uckfield, East Sussex,
TN22 1QQ England
Tel: +44 (0) 1825 749494
Fax: +44 (0) 1825 765701
www.naval-military-press.com

In reprinting in facsimile from the original, any imperfections are inevitably reproduced and the quality may fall short of modern type and cartographic standards.

NO. 30 SQUADRON.

ROYAL FLYING CORPS DETACHMENT EGYPT.

On the 4th November, 1914, a Detachment of the Royal Flying Corps as detailed below under the command of Captain S.D. Massy, 29th Punjabis, sailed from Avonmouth Docks for Egypt on "S.S.Beethoven" to co-operate with the Egyptian Army of Occupation :-

        Captain H.L.Reilly
        Second Lieutenant S.P.Cockerell
        1 Maurice Farman Shorthorn (1914 Type)
        2 "   "   (1913 Type)
        2 70 H.P. Renault Engines
        2 Crossley Light Tenders
        1 Leyland repair lorry
        2 Tent hangars (R.A.F. Pattern)
        Six months supply of petrol and oil for aircraft and mechanical transport.

(The two Maurice Farman 1913 Type were collected by Captain Reilly on 3.11.14. from the Aircraft Manufacturing Company, Hendon and taken by him to Avonmouth on that day).

The Detachment arrived at Alexandria on November 17th. Captain Massy proceeded to Cairo to discuss where the Detachment should be stationed. The Suez Canal is approximately 100 miles in length; the detachment being too small to split up and distribute along the canal, Ismailia was selected as the most central spot in the Canal zone from which to work, being midway on the Canal between Port Said and Suez from each of which place it was distant some 50 miles. It had good railway facilities and was the Headquarters of the Canal Defence Force operating under Major-General A.Wilson. (For the purpose of defence the canal was divided into three sectors: Suez to the Bitter Lakes, Deversoir, north of the Great Bitter Lake to El Ferdan and El Ferdan to Port Said). Ismailia, although so central, had one serious drawback in that if reconnaissances were required east of Port Said or Suez machines would have to fly 50 miles in either direction before commencing their reconnaissances.

Arrangements were also made on this day for the erection at Ismailia of one new double shed (each 60' x 40') and for the dismantling of 3 sheds (63' x 54', 60' x 51', 39' 39' x 36'.) at Heliopolis and their re-erection at Ismailia.

The detachment disembarked and entrained for Ismailia on the 18th. Difficulty was experienced in unloading and entraining material, the train being some 50 yards from the ship resulted in all goods having to be manhandled from ship to train.

Captain Massy proceeded to Heliopolis and took over two Henri Farman machines, (one of which was equipped with a 50 H.P. Gnome engine) and a 80 H.P. Gnome engine taken out of a Bleriot machine.

The detachment arrived at Camp Moascar, Ismailia, on 20th November, and the next few days were occupied in bringing up stores and machines to the camp and erecting hangars. On the 24th a landing ground, petrol and oil depot was established at Qantara on the east bank of the Suez Canal, midway between Ismailia and Port Said, in order to facilitate reconnaissance to Qatiya and places north-east of Qantara. For reconnaissances south and south-east in the direction of Wadi-el-Giddi and the Mitla Pass a similar depot was established at Suez on the

2nd December. These landing grounds were kept in order by the troops on the spot. B.Leonardi, an Italian Henri Farman pilot, joined for duty on the 26th and on the following day Captain L.V.A. Royle, Egyptian Coast Guards Administration, joined for duty as an observer. The erection of Maurice Farman No.369 having been completed on this day, the first reconnaissance flight was made by Lieutenant Cockerell with Captain Barlow as observer over Bir-el-Gilban and Bir Abu Abuk.

Captain W.F.Stirling joined for duty as observer on the 30th.

Captain Massy reported that weather conditions and visibility during November were excellent, and that at 4,000 feet over Ismailia on a clear day Port Said and Suez were visible.

December, 1914.

On the 1st December, Captain Reilly, observer Captain Stirling, made a two hour reconnaissance of Bir Abu Ramel, Qatiya, Hod Saadum, and Hod-el-Zeig.

A reconnaissance to Wadi-el-Giddi was made by Lieutenant Cockerell, observer Captain Royle on 2nd

On the 6th December, Maurice Farman No.712 was erected. A reconnaissance to Katra was made by Lieutenant Cockerell, observer Captain Royle. On the following day Captain Reilly, observer Captain Royle made a 4¾ hour reconnaissance of Ain el Sudr. Captain A.J. Ross, R.E. Egyptian Army, joined for duty as observer on the 9th. Maurice Farman No.369 was smashed on landing at Suez on the 15th due to bad ground. The pilot, Lieutenant Cockerell, sustained a broken left arm and the observer Captain Royle, was badly bruised. Maurice Farman No.713 was erected and flown on this day.

On the 21st Lieutenant S.C. Parr and three civilian mechanics arrived from the Indian Central Flying School with 1 B.E.2a (less engine) and 2 Maurice Farmans (1913 Type less engines). Captain W.F.Stirling was transferred to the French Seaplane Flight at Port Said. This flight consisted of seven seaplanes operating from Aenne Rickmers - a captured cargo steamer equipped as a seaplane carrier. These were put at the disposal of Sir John Maxwell by the French in November, 1914.

Captain G.B. Rickards and two N.C.O. pilots (Sergeants Foggin and Lilleywhite) joined from England with two Renault engines.

Lieutenant D.R. Tweedie, Egyptian Coast Guards, joined for duty as observer on the 26th and on the 30th a temporary petrol depot and advanced landing ground was established at Mabeiuk, and on the following day a similar depot was established at Ras el Hagg. These depots were made by troops who also carried out supplies of petrol and oil. From these depots reconnaissances were made to Bir el Hassana and Nekhl. Maurice Farman No.369 was rebuilt and flown on this day.

Captain Massy reports that the weather was more unsettled than during November. Flying was only possible after 8 a.m. during the first half owing to mists. During the latter half strong north-west winds and frequent sand storms were encountered.

January,
1915.

Second Lieutenant Sir J. Paul, Egyptian Irrigation Department, joined for duty as observer on 2.1.15. A reconnaissance to Qatiya was made on 6th by Captain Rickards with Lieutenant Paul as observer. Four days later the B.E. was erected and on the 12th Henri Farman No.1 was erected and flown.

The 15th saw an unsuccessful attempt made to establish an advanced temporary landing ground at Likleikha for a reconnaissance to Koaseima, but bad weather and a shelving beach made landing impossible.

An emergency landing ground and petrol depot was established at Qantara on the west bank of the canal on the 17th.

The Turkish Forces having been reported as possessing aircraft, a double company of Indian infantry was camped at the aerodrome for protection. This provided a firing party under a British officer and four look-out men with glasses. An aeroplane, pilot and observer detailed for the purpose were kept in constant readiness to take the air on the alarm being given.

A reconnaissance to Bir el Abd made by Captain Reilly, observer Lieutenant Tweedie on the 17th observed 720 Infantry, and 50 cavalry at Bir el Abd and 100 irregular cavalry at Bir Abu Raml all advancing on road to Qantara. On this occasion the aeroplane was fired upon and hit.

Lieutenants C.A.G. Mackintosh and H.G. Hillas, Egyptian Ministry of Finance, joined for duty as observers on the 18th. The following day Second Lieutenant F.O. Baxter, 2nd Rajputs, joined as observer. A reconnaissance flight was made on this day to Bir el Mahadat by Corporal W.B. Power, observer Captain Ross who reported "No signs of enemy".

On the 20th 1000 infantry and 200 cavalry were located and bombed at Bir el Abd by Captain Rickards, observer Lieutenant Tweedie.

Second Lieutenants K.L. Williams and B.G.N.B. Partridge, 2nd Rajputs, P.E.L. Gething and H.M. Ledger, 27th Punjabis, joined for duty as observers. Second Lieutenants Partridge and Gething were transferred to the French Seaplane Flight Port Said on the 23rd.

On the 25th reconnaissances were made to Bir el Mahadat, W. Sudr and Mabeiuk and Birl el Abd. On the latter reconnaissance Corporal Power, observer Lieutenant Tweedie made a forced landing on the coat owing to engine trouble. The machine barely managed to escape from a Turkish cavalry patrol of 300. The machine was heavily shelled with shrapnel. On the same day 2000 infantry were observed 2 miles S.E. of Bir el Mahadat, 3600 at Bir el Mabeiuk and 1000 infantry and 300 cavalry six miles from Qantara. On the 27th a large body of troops ready to move were observed at Moiya Harab; these were bombed, and also 2000 infantry at Wadi Muksheib, and 3000 infantry and 300 cavalry 15 miles N.E. of Ismailia.

On the 28th the B.E.2a was smashed as a result of a forced landing at Nefisha. Second Lieutenant Sir R.J. Paul and Lieutenant H.G. Hillas were transferred to the French Seaplane Flight.

Second Lieutenants K.L. Williams, F.O. Baxter, 2nd Rajputs, and H.M.G. Ledger, 27th Punjabis, transferred to French Seaplane Flight on 30th and reconnaissances made to Dueidar, Ghabeita and Aiyun Musa and El Rigum.

The weather during January was generally worse than in December owing to heavy low clouds and haze. 25 reconnaissances were carried out during the month and the average number of machines available 3.

February, 1915.

From the enemy's movements observed during January, it was evident that an attack was imminent. This materialised on the 3rd February and was mainly directed against the central sector of the canal i.e. El Ferdan to Deversoir but was completely repulsed by the 6th. On the 5th it was observed and reported that the enemy were retiring towards Qatiya and that those opposite the central sector were concentrated east of Bir Habeita in their old camp on which bombs were dropped.

On the opening day of the attack five and a half hours were spent in aerial reconnaissance and fourteen hours on the fifth. The G.O.C. of the Canal Defence Force being constantly informed of the disposition, movements and strength of the enemy.

On the 7th General Sir J. Maxwell wired to the G.O.C. of the Canal Defence Forces :-

"Will you please convey to Captain Massy and the officers of the Royal Flying Corps, also the observers, my appreciation of the hard and good work they have done with inferior machines. I do not know what we should have done without them" and General Wilson in his despatch of the 11th February said:-

"In conclusion, I desire to express my high appreciation of the valuable work done by the pilots and observers of the French hydroplane squadron and the detachment Royal Flying Corps in the numerous reconnaissances carried out by them previous to and during the advance of the enemy. They were constantly under shrapnel and rifle fire and carried out their difficult and dangerous duties with courage, resourcefulness and courage".

On the 11th an electric searchlight plant was installed at Ismailia in view of a possible attempt at a night raid over enemy camps. The plant consisted of two direct coupled steam engines and generators. The steam engines were disconnected and the generators driven by belts from counter shafts on the repair lorry platform, the counter shaft being driven by a belt from the brake drum of the lorry, the back wheels being jacked up. This provided current for two 20 inch projectors.

The Henri Farman machine No.2 was erected on the 20th and two days later the B.E.2a smashed at Nefisha was re-erected.

On the 28th a temporary advanced landing ground was established at El Rigum for reconnaissances to Bir el Themada and Gebel el Maghara.

Reconnaissances were undertaken on 23 out of the 28 days of the month, a total number of 41 reconnaissances were made, the average number of machines available being 4.

March, 1915.

During March twenty-six reconnaissances were carried out including five to Mitla and one to El Murra. The latter being the longest single flight made by the Detachment and was carried out by Captain Reilly, observer Captain Royle in the B.E.2a machine. A distance of 176 miles was covered and 3 hours 28 minutes spent in the air. In order to make this flight a specially large petrol tank was fitted into the machine. On arrival some 207 tents and 300 infantry were located and bombed. The aeroplane was fired at but the observer failed to locate the gun or guns.

On the 26th a temporary advanced landing ground was prepared at Qatiya by the Bikanir Camel Corps for reconnaissances to El Murra and El Mazar.

The detachment suffered the loss on the 20th of Second Lieutenant S.P. Cockerell who died of acute smallpox.

Lieutenant S.C. Parr and the four mechanics from the Indian Central School left the detachment for the Indian Expeditionary Force, Mesopotamia on the 30th.

The small number of reconnaissances carried out during March in comparison to those in February was due to bad weather, rain and sand storms prevented flying for a week in the middle of the month.

April, 1915.

In April the detachment had the following machines on charge:-

Machine	No.	Type	Notes
Maurice Farman	No.369	1914 Type	) Brought with detachment from England.
" "	No.712	1913 "	)
" "	No.713	" "	)
Henri Farman	No.1		) Acquired in Heliopolis Nov. 1914.
" "	No.2		)
B.E.2.a.			Received from India Dec. 1914.
B.E.2.c.	No.1757		Received from England in April, 1915.

The two Maurice Farmans 1913 Type received from India in December were dispatched to the Indian Expeditionary Force "D" (Mesopotamia) during April.

Total strength of detachment on the 30th April was 4 Officers and 44 Other Ranks.

Fifty nine reconnaissances were made during the month and 5,600 miles flown. Total hours spent in the air 116.

On the 16th, using Qatiya as an intermediate landing ground a bombing raid was made on El Murra by Sergeant Foggin, observer Captain Conran in Maurice Farman No.712 Lieutenant Murray, observer Captain Royle in the B.E.2a, and Captain Rickards, observer Lieutenant Tweedie in Maurice Farman No.713. All reached the objective. Captain Massy's report of the raid is as follows:

"On the 16th April five machines left Ismailia at "five a.m. and landed at Catia where an advanced landing ground

"and petrol depot had been established by a patrol of the
"Bikanir Camel Corps. Of the above four were fitted with
"bomb frames and carried three bombs each. It was intended
"to send these four machines from Qatiya to El Murra to locate
"and bomb an aeroplane shed which had been previously reported
"as having been erected there. Actually only three of the
"four machines started from and returned to Qatiya. The
"fourth developed engine trouble at Qatiya and could not be
"got going before the first machine had been and returned from
"El Murra. It finally had to return to Ismailia without
"passenger or bombs. No reconnaissance report was of course
"written out for this machine. The fifth machine which was
"not fitted with a bomb frame remained at Qatiya with a view
"to going out and searching for any overdue machines. All
"three returned safely, however, to Qatiya. The engine of
"one machine was in serious trouble on its return to Qatiya
"but I considered it just possible for it to make Qantara on
"the way back which it actually did, landing there with a
"broken connecting rod cylinder and bottom half of crank case
"due to the white metal running in the big end.

" The distances as the crow flies are as follows:-

" Ismailia to Qatia   42 miles
" Qatia to El Murra and back   124 miles
" Qatia to Ismailia   42 miles.

"Seven out of nine bombs carried were dropped, two
"failing to leave the bomb frame. The camp appeared to be
"laid out with the object of suffering as little damage as
"possible from aircraft but all pilots and observers were
"unanimous in their opinion that what was supposed to have
"been the aeroplane shed could not possibly have been so."

On the 28th an enemy camp was located at Hawawish,
13 miles east of the Canal at a point midway between Ismailia
and El Ferdan. Brigadier-General W.A.Watson, with a column
consisting of eight squadrons of the Imperial Service Cavalry
Brigade, a half battalion of 27th Punjabis and a section of
Egyptian Artillery left Ismailia that night with the intention
of surprising him. The Turkish force, however, moved while
it was dark and made an attack on Bench Mark Post which was
easily repulsed. It then retired but was again located by
aeroplanes the following morning at Bir el Mahadat not far
from its former position.

May,
1915.

During May 34 reconnaissances were carried out,
approximately 4,900 miles flown, and a total of 91 hours
spent in the air. The average number of machines available
being 4.

An agent reported during the month that a determined
effort was to be made to burn down the aeroplane sheds, in
consequence of which the sheds were surrounded by a barbed
wire fence along which at intervals electric light standards
were erected. Guards were doubled and two men were detailed
to sleep in each shed.

On the 26th Maurice Farman No.369 piloted by
Sergeant Power, observer Captain Conran returning from a
reconnaissance to Baiyud and Mageibra crashed into the Canal
2 miles north of El Ferdan. The machine struck the water
nose down at extreme speed and was completely wrecked. The
pilot and observer swam ashore, sustaining bruises and a
broken rib and bruises and cuts on the head respectively.

Copy extract from A.H. 15/231/13.

87/4469/M.A.1.

31st July, 1915.

The Officer Commanding,
    No. 30 Squadron,
        Royal Flying Corps,
            Egypt.

       With reference to your letter of 10th instant, No.1/496, I am directed to inform you that the detachment of the Royal Flying Corps under your command became No.30 Squadron on 24th March, 1915.

            (Sgd.) S.MacSwiney Major for
                      Major, Gen. Staff
     For Deputy Director of Military Aeronautics.

June, 1915.	Twenty-three reconnaissances were made during June 2,900 miles flown. These reconnaissances were carried out mostly between 4 a.m. and 9 a.m., owing to the intense heat prevailing later during the day. Observation was often marred by dense clouds prevailing from dawn to 7.30 a.m. at heights varying from 800-2500 feet.
July, 1915.	Twenty-seven reconnaissances were made during July and 2821 miles flown. The average number of machines available was 4; signalling and photography was commenced by the detachment this month. 3 Signalling and 4 photographic flights were made. The first photographic flight being made on the 19th by Sergeant Froggin, observer Captain Conran in Maurice Farman 712 and the first signalling flight on the 25th. Second Lieutenant J.R.McCrindle joined for duty on the 30th. On 31st Major Massy was informed that the detachment under his command become No.30 Squadron with effect from 24th March, 1915.
August, 1915.	14 Reconnaissances were made and 1833 miles flown during August. Captain Conran ceased to be attached as observer on the 24th. Captain E.H.M.O'Farrell, Egyptian Army, joined as observer on the following day. On the 29th Martinsyde Scout No.4250 arrived from Alexandria.
September, 1915.	During September 15 reconnaissances were made 1834 miles flown. The average number of machines available being 4. Command of the squadron taken over by Captain G.B. Rickards.
October, 1915.	Thirteen reconnaissances were made in October, 1359 miles flown. The average number of machines being 4. Photographs taken on all reconnaissances. B.E's 4711 and 4712 arrived from England on the 2nd. Captain J.W Thomson-Glover joined as observer on the 14th And on the following day Lieutenant E.A. Floyer joined as observer.
November, 1915.	From 1st to 26.11.15, sixteen reconnaissances were made, and 1961 miles flown. Average number of machines available five. On the 26th November No.30 Squadron was relieved by "A" Flight of No.14 Squadron which had arrived at Alexandria with the 5th Wing on the 19th. 5 Officers (observers) and 7 Other Ranks were transferred from No.30 to No.14 Squadron and the flight took over all machines. On the 9th December the personnel of No.30 Squadron were ordered to proceed to Basra. Captain G.B. Rickards, Lieutenants Clogstoun and Davidson, Captain Thomson-Glover and a portion of the flight arrived at Basra on 27.12.15 and become "C" Flight of No.30 Squadron.

Copy extract from A.H. 204/11/150.

20/R.F.C/75 (M.A.1.) War Office,
London, S.W.
11th August, 1915.

The Officer Commanding,
    Administrative Wing,
        Royal Flying Corps,
            South Farnborough.

With reference to your letter dated 3rd instant, I am directed to inform you that the Flight, Royal Flying Corps, in Egypt, is a part of No.30 Squadron.

I am further to inform you, that certain proposals have been placed before the Government of India, and if these are agreed to, the flights at present in Mesopotamia will become the other two flights of this squadron.

(Sgd.) H.P.R. Coode   Captain
for Deputy Director of Military Aeronautics.

Copy extract from AH/204/11/150.

30th September, 1915.

List of officers serving with Detachment of
No.30 Squadron, Egypt.

Flight Commander:-	Capt. G.B.Rickards	Special Reserve
Flying Officers :-	Lieut.H.P.S.Clogstoun	Special Reserve
	2nd Lieut.Viscount Exmouth (In Hospital, Ismailia since 7.9.15).	7th Battalion Royal Berkshire Regiment
	2nd Lieut,J.R.McCrindle	7th Battn.Gordon Highlanders (T.F.)
Observers :-	Capt. A.J. Ross	Royal Engineers
	Capt.E.H.M.O'Farrell	Royal Irish Regt. (att.Egyptian Army)
	Lieut.C.A.G.Mackintosh	Temporary commission for duty as observer.

Copy extract from A.H. 204/11/150.

30th October, 1915.

List of Officers serving with Egypt Detachment
No.30 Squadron.

Flight Commander:-	Capt. G.B.Rickards	Special Reserve
Flying Officers :-	Capt. L.Wanless O'Gowan	2nd Battalion Scottish Rifles
	Lieut. H.P.S.Clogstoun	Special Reserve
	2nd Lieut. J.R.McCrindle	7th Bn. Gordon Highlanders
	2nd Lieut. Viscount Exmouth (on sick leave)	7th Bn. Royal Berkshire Regt.
	2nd Lieut. D.A.L.Davidson	Special Reserve
Assistant Equipment Officer:-	Lieut. S.C.Parr	Royal Flying Corps
Observers :-	Capt. A.J. Ross	Royal Engineers
	Capt. E.H.M.O'Farrell	Royal Irish Regt. (att. Egyptian Army).
	Capt. J.W.Thomson-Glover	35th Sikhs (att. 92nd Punjabis).
	Lieut. E.A. Floyer	I.A.R.O.
	Lieut. R.C. Carver	Temporary Commission.

Copy extract from A.H. 204/11/150.

30th November, 1915.

List of Officers serving with Egypt Detachment
No.30 Squadron.

Flight Commander:-	Capt. G.B.Rickards	Special Reserve
Flying Officers :-	Capt. L.Wanless O'Gowan	2nd Battn. Scottish Rifles
	Lieut. H.P.S.Clogstoun	Special Reserve
	2nd Lieut. J.R.McCrindle	7th Bn. Gordon Highlanders T.F.
	2nd Lieut. Viscount Exmouth (on sick leave)	7th Bn. Royal Berks Regt.
	2nd Lieut. D.A.L.Davidson	Special Reserve
Assistant Equipment Officer:-	Lieut. S.C.Parr	Royal Flying Corps.

MESOPOTAMIA.

March 1915.

The original air unit in Mesopotamia was mobilised and maintained by the Government of India, and comprised personnel from India, Australia, New Zealand and England.

The following organisation was provided:-

A Flight in the field supported by a Park and a Depot in Bombay.

16/3/23.

The Flight under a Flight Commander was equipped as a field unit with tools, stores and power repair plant, and water transport supplemented with a small amount of land transport.

The Park was provided with repair plant, tools and equipment. The functions of this unit were to receive all personnel and equipment and to undertake such overhauls and reconstruction of aeroplanes which could not be carried out by the Flight.

Captain P.W.L. Broke-Smith, Royal Engineers, was appointed Deputy Assistant Director of Aviation on the Staff of the G.O.C. Indian Expeditionary Force "D" ("D" being the letter allotted to the Expeditionary Force in Mesopotamia) in March 1915, to organise and administer the flying service in Mesopotamia.

209/24/4.

Captain H.L. Reilly, 82nd Punjabis, was appointed to command the Flight in April and a Public Works Department Engineer Officer, W.R. Wills, Esq., who was experienced in aeroplanes was appointed engineer in March with the rank of Second Lieutenant, Indian Army Reserve of Officers.

April 1915.

Captain Broke-Smith arrived at Basra from Bombay on the 9th April. The Park was established at Basra and a site for the aerodrome selected at Mekina Malsus, some two miles N.W. of Basra, but had to be vacated owing to floods. Eventually the base aerodrome was established at Tanumah on the left bank of the Shat al Arab opposite Basra.

Captain Reilly and Lieutenant Wills arrived at Basra from Bombay on the 30th.

May 1915.

On the 14th May, Captain H.A. Petre, Australian Flying Corps and Lieutenant W.A. Burn, New Zealand Staff Corps arrived with 2 Maurice Farmans (1 Longhorn, 1 Shorthorn, 70 H.P. Renault engines which had arrived at Bombay from England on 27th of April), 11 Other Ranks (British) 5 Indian mechanics and 10 followers.

Captain T. White and Lieutenant W.H. Treloar, Australian Flying Corps, arrived on the 20th with 20 W.O's, N.C.O's and men and 2 Maurice Farmans (without engines) which had been sent from Egypt.

16/3/23.

209/24/4

209/24/5

To avoid confusion with the Turkish Emblem (crescent within circle) it was decided that our aeroplanes should be marked with a black stripe in place of the red dot inside a blue circle.

The first practice flight was carried out on the 27th. Major Reilly flying the Maurice Farman Shorthorn with Major Broke-Smith made a 35 minute flight reaching an altitude of 4,800 feet and ascertaining that the speed of the machine was 55 miles an hour.

On the 30th an advanced landing ground and filling station was established at Chirish, 1½ miles south of Qurna in order to enable the flight to co-operate with the military forces who were commencing operations from Qurna on the following day.

During the battle of Qurna, Major Reilly, observer Major Broke-Smith in the Maurice Farman Longhorn, and Captain Petre, observer Lieutenant Burn in the Maurice Farman Shorthorn reconnoitred the Turkish positions on the Tigris to Sakrikiya some 10 miles north of Qurna.

June 1915.
209/24/5.

On the 1st June a mobile flight base with aeroplane tents was established at Bahrein so that the flight might keep up with the Army who were pursuing the Turks in the direction of Amara. Prior to the establishment of this base the flight had been compelled to return to Basra each night.

209/61/1

The flight started as a separate unit from the depot at Basra on the 3rd June. It consisted of 4 Officers, 2 Maurice Farmans, one stores tug (T.3.) with a crew of 23 and 13 British mechanics. 20 men of the 120th Infantry were attached to and accompanied the flight to Abu Rabah thence to Amara.

On the 1st and 2nd June the flight co-operated in the pursuit of the Turks to Amara, a distance of 50 miles from the refilling point at Bahrein, reporting on the enemy's movements and the extent and limit of floods adjacent to the Tigris.

Amara was occupied on the 4th and a refilling point established there on the following day.

Lieutenant G.P. Merz, Australian Corps, joined for duty on the 13th.

16/3/23.

A notable reconnaissance from Amara to Kut al Amara, a distance of 123 miles by air, was made on the 14th by Major Reilly, observer Lieutenant Burn to locate the enemy's dispositions at and below Kut al Amara. A refilling point at Ali Gharbi some 60 miles from Amara was utilised on this occasion. A sketch map made at the time was subsequently used by Major-General Townshend for his plans on the attack on Kut al Amara. At the conclusion of this reconnaissance the flight returned to Basra.

209/24/6

In view of the forthcoming operations against Nasiriya, a filling point was established on the 20th at Abu Salabik, an island 4 miles N.E. of Ghabishiya, 45 miles from Basra, from which on the 22nd Maurice Farman No.1 (Shorthorn) set out to reconnoitre Nasiriya and Maurice Farman No.2 (Longhorn) the Hammar Lake. The latter was successful but the former was compelled to land by magneto trouble ten miles from the filling point. The reconnaissance was effected, however, on the following day by transferring the magneto from Maurice Farman No.2.

July 1915.	Captain B.S. Atkins joined for duty as an observer on July 3rd.
209/24/7.	Two Caudron biplanes (60 H.P. Gnome engines) arrived on the 14th and were numbered 3 and 4.
209/61/2.	On the 18th the flight personnel (less aeroplanes, pilots and observers) left Basra with tug T.3 towing flight lighter and bellum to proceed through Qurna to Asani.
209/24/7.	On the 19th the two Caudrons left Basra for Asani. Caudron No.4 arrived safely, Caudron No.3 did not arrive until the 22nd owing to a forced landing en route and having had to await a new engine from Basra.
209/24/7. 21/6/87.	Reconnaissances of the Turkish positions at Nasiriya were carried out on the 21st and 22nd, and on 22nd and 23rd Major Reilly ranged the artillery on enemy trenches. General reconnaissance work was carried out until the 25th.
21/6/87.	General Sir John Nixon, Commanding Indian Expeditionary Force (D) stated in his despatch :- "I have to place on record the excellence of the "work performed by officers and men of the Royal Flying Corps, "whose valuable reconnaissances materially assisted in "clearing up the situation before the battle of the 24th July".
209/61/3.	On the 30th both Caudrons set out for Basra. C.3 arrived on the 31st after two forced landings, but C.4 piloted by Lieutenant Merz with Lieutenant Burn as observer, was reported missing. Lieutenant Treloar with Sergeant Heath in Maurice Farman No.1 went out in search immediately. The machine was eventually located by Major Reilly and Captain Petre on the 2nd August where it had forced landed 25 miles west of Abu Salabik. Both the pilot and observer were missing and the machine had been damaged by the Arabs. It was subsequently ascertained that Lieutenants Merz and Burn had been killed by a party of Zobaah after a running fight of four miles.
	Caudron No.4 was dismantled and brought back to Basra by water where it arrived on the 8th August.
August 1915.	The flight was now required for the Tigris operation and so all personnel, flight lighter and bellum were withdrawn from Asani on the 3rd August arriving at Basra on the following day.
	Maurice Farman No.2 was handed over to the Park on the 21st for instructional purposes, with Captain Petre as instructor.
209/24/8.	Caudron No.3 and Maurice Farman No.1 arrived at Amara on the 25th having been towed up from Basra on the platform lighter by the tug "Shirin".
	The flight was re-inforced during August by the arrival of 3 - 70 H.P. Renault engines from England and 4 Martinsyde Scout biplanes with 3 - 80 H.P. Gnome engines from Australia. A second lighter was taken over and fitted as a workshop. The flight had now a workshop and stores lighter one of which was fitted with a dark room and photographic equipment.

From 26th to 31st August the flight at Amara carried out practice in Artillery observation by means of Very lights, smoke balls and electric signal lamps.

209/24/8.

209/61/3

16/3/23.

Intimation was received in August that the provision of flying units in Mesopotamia would be taken over by the War Office and that the flight would now become part of No.30 Squadron, a flight of which had already been formed in Egypt and which would be transferred to Mesopotamia in the forthcoming November. All demands for aircraft and equipment were now to be made direct to England.

21/6/27.

With effect from the 5th August all officers of the unit were gazetted to the Royal Flying Corps.

September 1915.

On the 6th September the flight left Amara for Ali Gharbi with the following machines on the platform lighter:-

Maurice Farman (M.F.) No.1.
Caudron (C). No.3.
Martinsydes (M.H.) Nos. 5 and 6,

the two latter having arrived from Basra on the 5th.

Maurice Farman No.1 was wrecked on landing from the lighter at Ali Gharbi on the 9th and was returned to Basra.

209/61/4.

A reconnaissance to Shaikh Saad on the 13th reported "all clear" and it was occupied by the Army on the following day.

M.H.5 was wrecked soon after taking off for reconnaissance duty on the 14th. Later in the day Major Reilly on M.H.6 reconnoitred the Turkish positions at Es Sinn near Kut al Amara.

An aerial reconnaissance to Es Sinn was commenced on the 16th by Lieutenant Treloar and Captain Atkins in C.3. The machine was shot down by rifle fire and both officers were made prisoners.

The flight was now left with one machine, the Martinsyde Scout (M.H.6) on which Major Reilly successfully completed the reconnaissance the same evening bringing back detailed information of the enemy trench system and map. The flight then moved to Sannaiyat.

209/24/9.

A R.N.A.S. Seaplane Flight from East Africa had now arrived at Basra under the command of Major R. Gordon consisting of 4 officers, 1 W.O., 21 N.C.O's. and men and 4 150 H.P. Sunbeam Short Seaplanes.

Two seaplanes and Maurice Farman No.7 and Martinsyde Scout No.8 arrived at Sannaiyat from Amara on 23rd.

On the 26th September the flight moved up from Sannaiyat to Nukhailat. Captain Petre on M.H.8 crashed on landing. The following machines were now available for the battle of Kut al Amara :-

2 Short Seaplanes.
1 Maurice Farman.
1 Martinsyde Scout.

On the 28th during the battle the seaplanes which were fitted with Stirling (30 mile radius) wireless sets were attached to the artillery for observation. Lieutenant Fulton, observer Captain Yeats Brown on M.F.7 and Major Reilly on M.H.6 carried out continuous reconnaissances during the day watching and reporting enemy movements and maintaining communication between the 6th Division Headquarters at Nukhailat and General Delemain's column operating against the enemy's left flank in the vicinity of Suwada Marsh. This column would otherwise have been out of touch, telegraphic communication having broken down at 11 a.m.

209/24/9.
16/3/23.
21/6/87.

The flight moved to Kut al Amara on the 30th.

16/3/23.

The subsequent movements of the enemy in retreat up the Tigris from Kut al Amara past Aziziya as far as Ctesiphon were observed daily until the 6th of October.

October 1915.
16/3/23.

On the 3rd October Major Reilly reconnoitred Ctesiphon from Kut al Amara reporting that the Turks were already strongly entrenched in prepared positions.

209/61/5.

On the 5th Major Reilly flew the M.H.6 to Aziziya and on the same evening again reconnoitred the Ctesiphon position. On the following day M.H.8 and M.F.7 arrived at Aziziya.

209/61/5.

The first reconnaissance to Baghdad was carried out by Captain Petre on the 6th in M.H.8 which unfortunately crashed on landing.

209/61/5.

M.F.2 arrived from Amara on the 19th. On the 22nd a bombing raid was carried out by three machines on a hostile Arab village 5 miles south west of Frasers Post. Sixteen 2 lb., two 20 lb. Hales H.E. and three 30 lb. bombs were dropped. On the 27th the village flew the white flag.

16/3/23.

The work of the flight until the end of the month consisted of locating the enemy's dispositions at and below Ctesiphon, watching the country to the flanks of the Lines of Communications north and south of Kut al Amara and maintaining touch between the 6th Division Headquarters at Aziziya and G.H.Q. at Kut al Amara.

Two of the seaplanes were converted to land machines during October.

Meanwhile the following reinforcements had arrived at Basra:- 1 Equipment officer, 2 Assistant Equipment officers, and the personnel of a complete Repair Section Aircraft Park with 2 repair lorries, also Captains F.M.Murray and S.C.Winfield-Smith, 2 B.E.2C's and eight men which were to form part of the second flight.

November 1915.

On November the 5th there arrived from England Major R.A. Bradley and Lieutenant A. Graves, 25 N.C.O's and men and a further 2 B.E.2C's and stores to complete the second flight.

On the 7th the personnel was distributed into Headquarters No.30 Squadron, "A" and "B" Flights and No.4 Aircraft Park. The original flight with its personnel became "A" Flight. "B" Flight was composed of the personnel recently arrived from England, and Headquarters, of the remaining personnel including the mule transport establishment and M.T. drivers.

"B" Flight left Basra for Aziziya on the 9th November on flight lighters towed by Tug T.3. It consisted of Captain Murray and Lieutenant Graves, two B.E.2C's (Nos.11 and 12) and 22 N.C.O's and men. On the 15th the tug grounded twelve miles above Kut the aeroplanes were disembarked, erected and flown to Aziziya.

On the 13th Captain White, observer Captain Yeats-Brown in M.F.2 landed and attempted to cut the telegraph wires north and west of Baghdad, but were taken prisoners. Both officers subsequently escaped.

B.E.2C No.11, M.H.8 and the two converted seaplanes flew from Aziziya to Lajj on the 20th. The B.E.2C was wrecked on landing.

During the day Major Reilly on M.H.6 was shot down by machine gun fire whilst on reconnaissance behind the Turkish lines and made prisoner.

21/13/892.
In a staff monograph on the Battle of Ctesiphon, Staff Bimbashi Mehemet Emin, formerly Head of the Section of Military Movements, Turkish Army, writes as follows concerning Major Reilly's capture:-

"An event which occurred that day (20th November, "1915) had an effect out of proportion with reality. After "midday an aeroplane flying at a height of 1000 metres in a "last attempt to examine our lines of defences and rear, "was brought down and captured by means of machine gun fire "from the 51st Division. This little event was taken as a "happy omen that the luck of the enemy was about to change.... "it caused a deeply felt improvement in the general morale. "The presence of the 51st Division which turned the balance "of success against the assailants in this battle was ascer-"tained on this fruitless reconnaissance and was shewn on the "airman's map.

"But the map containing this priceless information "fell, not into the hands of the enemy commander awaiting "anxiously for it before making his last dispositions, "but into those of the Osmanli commander.............

"Major Reilly's greatest gift to us was the sketch "showing the course of the Tigris from the Diala to Aziziya. "This little sketch, probably of small account to the enemy, "was an important map in the eyes of the Iraq command. For "at H.Q. and with the troops there was no such thing as a "map."

After the capture of Major Reilly, Major R. Gordon, R.N.A.S., took over command of the flight which consisted of one Maurice Farman, one Martinsyde Scout and the two converted seaplanes.

21/6/87.
The Battle of Ctesiphon commenced on the 22nd and on the opening day Lieutenant Fulton on the Martinsyde forced landed behind the enemy's lines and was made prisoner.

209/24/11.
This left M.F.7 the only aeroplane in working order.

Two machines only were in action throughout the 22nd, a converted Short seaplane and Maurice Farman 7.

M.F.7 with the two Short seaplanes were in action during the morning of the 24th with the addition of a B.E.2c, in the afternoon. Seven reconnaissance flights were made and messages dropped on 6th Division Headquarters.

During the battle the general work of the aeroplanes consisted of :-

(A) Watching both flanks and looking out for enveloping movements.

21/6/87.

(B) Reporting on the enemy's dispositions and movements.

209/24/11.

(C) Observing the enemy's rear along both banks of the Tigris to above the Diyala river junction, to look out for movements of reinforcements and reserves or signs of retreat.

16/3/23.

(D) Locating enemy's guns - particularly the heavy gun battery near Seleucia (this commanded the river below the bend at Bustan and prevented the Naval flotilla from moving up and co-operating; it also prevented troops approaching the river to fetch water except by night.

(E) Bombing with 100 lb. bombs masses of enemy troops in rear and boat bridge across the Diyala river.

(F) Noting the moves of the Naval flotilla.

Major S.D. Massy arrived at Kut al Amara on the 28th November and assumed command of No.30 Squadron. On the same day the four machines (2 Short converted seaplanes, B.E.2c and Maurice Farman) returned to Kut from Aziziya.

The converted seaplanes were returned to Basra early in December to refit.

209/22/7.
December 1915.

On the 1st December there were no machines available for reconnaissance work, all being under repair.

At the end of November the composition of No.30 Squadron was as follows:-

Commanding Officer.

Major S.D. Massy.

Equipment Officer.

Captain W.R. Wills.

"A" Flight.

Flight Commander :- Captain H.A. Petre.
Flying Officers :- Captain T.R. Wills.
Observers :- Captain S.C.B. Munday.
Lieutenant C.H.C. Munro.

"B" Flight.

Flight Commander :- Captain E.M. Murray.
Flying Officers :- Captain S.C. Winfield Smith.
Lieutenant A. Graves.
Observers :- Captain R.D. de la C. Corbett.
Lieutenant G.A.R. Spain.

Machines.

"A" Flight.	"B" Flight.
M.F. Shorthorn No.1 (70 H.P. Renault)	B.E.2c No.11 (90 H.P. R.A.F.)
M.F. Longhorn No.7 (" " ")	" No.12A (" " ")
Martinsyde Scout No.M.H.9 (80 H.P. Gnome)	" No.14 (" " ")

209/22/7.
    Orders were issued on the 6th December by the General Staff 6th Division for as many machines as could fly to move out of Kut on the following day to Ali Gharbi: Captain Petre with Major Massy and Captain Murray with Lieutenant Spain on M.F.1 and B.E.2c respectively flew to Ali Gharbi on the 7th. There remained in Kut, two damaged B.E.2c's, one damaged Martinsyde, Captains Wills and Winfield Smith, and observers Captains Corbett and Munday and Lieutenant Munro, also the majority of the rank and file of "A" and "B" Flights and "A" Flight Lighters. On this day the investment of Kut al Amara by the Turks was complete.

    On the 16th the Squadron Depot under Captain W.R. Wills was moved from Basra to Amara. After establishing this Depot Major Massy returned to Ali Gharbi on the 18th with one Maurice Farman Longhorn.

    A few reconnaissance flights were carried out during the remaining days of December to report the dispositions and strength of the enemy forces enveloping Kut al Amara.

209/24/2.
    Captain G.B. Rickards Commanding the Flight from Egypt with Flying Officers Captain L. Wanless O'Gowan, Lieutenant H.P.S. Clogstoun, Second Lieutenants D.A.L. Davidson and Second Lieutenant J.R. McGrindle and observers Captain J.W. Thomson-Glover with a portion of the Flight arrived at Basra on the 27th where it remained to equip. It was designated "C" Flight of No.30 Squadron.

January 1916.
Mespot.
Campaign
Vol.II
Page 200.
    From the 1st to the 5th of January the only available machine was M.F.1. On the 1st General Townshend reported the advent of the first hostile aeroplane over Kut apparently engaged on reconnaissance work. A few days later General Townshend heard from a Turkish deserter that four Turkish aeroplanes had arrived at Baghdad.

21/6/87.
    The first attempt to relieve Kut commenced on the 4th January when the leading troops of the 7th Division under General Younghusband, advanced from Ali Gharbi towards Shaikh Saad. The flights continuously moved up with the advancing troops, operating successively from Ali Gharbi, Musandag, Shaikh Saad arriving at Ora on the 16th where they remained until the end of the month.

209/22/8.
    There were now two machines available M.F.1 and a B.E.2c. In spite of adverse weather conditions in which the aeroplanes remained out night and day, when opportunities for keeping them in flying trim were few, reconnaissances were carried out daily until the end of the month.

21/6/87.
    On the 24th six photographs were taken of the enemy's front position, and movements behind the position at Es Sinn were reported together with numbers of troops located.

On the 17th January two 140 H.P. Voisin biplanes arrived at Basra for the use of the R.N.A.S. As the R.N.A.S. were short of officers and the R.F.C. had the personnel of a flight that had arrived from Egypt without machines, a composite Flight drawn from the R.N.A.S. and R.F.C. was formed during January consisting of two 150 H.P. Short biplanes and two 140 H.P. Voisin biplanes for duty with the Tigris Corps. One Short biplane and one Voisin joined No.30 Squadron at Ora on the 3rd February.

After the arrival of the R.N.A.S. machines and stores, the Maurice Farman equipment and the nucleus of "A" Flight were sent down to Basra to re-equip with B.E.2c's which were en route from England leaving a B.E.2c, the only R.F.C. machine with No.30 Squadron.

February 1916.
21/6/87.
209/22/9.

During the month of February, in addition to reconnaissance and artillery observation work, frequent flights were made to Kut al Amara for the purpose of dropping stores, spare parts for wireless plant, medical comforts and money both in cash and notes.

The following machines arrived at Basra during February:-

209/24/14.

Five 225 H.P. Sunbeam Short tractor seaplanes. Two 140 H.P. Canton Unne, Henri Farman Voisin biplanes	Arrived on 12th for R.N.A.S.
Four B.E.2c's allotted to 'A' Flight 6 Lewis guns for R.F.C. and 6 for R.N.A.S.	Arrived on 21st.

March 1916.

The strength of the R.F.C. at Ora on the 1st March was one B.E.2c belonging to 'B' Flight. The squadron was reinforced by one B.E.2c on the 5th, another on the 7th. On the 8th "A" Flight joined from Basra with a further two B.E.2c's.

H.F.Voisin No.1541, piloted by Lieutenant R.H.Peck, observer Captain W.G. Palmer, was shot down by machine gun fire whilst over Es Sinn on the 5th the pilot and observer being killed. A message to this effect was dropped by a Turkish aeroplane on the following day.

On the 6th instructions were issued by G.H.Q. Indian Expeditionary Force "D" that :- "Wing Commander R.Gordon, R.N.A.S. will, as senior officer, act as Aircraft Commander Tigris Column, and the two squadrons (1 R.N.A.S. and 1 R.F.C.) attached to this column will be under his orders".

The R.N.A.S. Unit was now organised into two flights. One, the original flight, was equipped with aeroplanes and the other with seaplanes which had arrived in February.

"B" Flight returned to Basra to refit on the 11th.

209/24/15.

Thirteen B.E.2c's arrived at Basra from England on the 20th.

General reconnaissance work was carried out during the month and further supplies dropped into Kut al Amara.

209/22/11.
April 1916.
        On the 1st April 1916 the squadron was located at Camp Wadi, and comprised "A" Flight with four B.E.2c's. Captain Murray and Lieutenant Clogstoun with "B" Flight personnel with three B.E.2c's joined the squadron from Basra on the 11th.

        On the 16th instructions were received for the dropping of as much food as possible into Kut. Bomb frames were removed from all machines and replaced by hastily devised dropping gear. Each machine carried 150 pounds of food per journey. Some sixty one food dropping flights were made from 17th to 28th April and combined with the R.N.A.S. Squadron 19,000 lbs. of food were dropped of which Kut acknowledged the receipt of 16,800 lbs.

        On the 19th Captain Wanless O'Gowan and Lieutenant Merton joined the Squadron from Basra with a Maurice Farman and a B.E.2c. Lieutenant Walmsley and Captain Truman arrived with Maurice Farmans on the 22nd and 26th respectively.

        Whilst returning from a food dropping flight on 26th Lieutenant Davidson was attacked by a hostile monoplane and wounded in the shoulder. The machine was hit in thirty two places. Escorts were in future provided.

209/24/16.

21/6/87.

209/22/12.
        By the 30th "C" Flight with three Maurice Farmans was complete at Squadron Headquarters, but had to return to Basra on the 4th of May owing to the three Maurice Farmans being wrecked in a storm. Three B.E.2c's and one Maurice Farman arrived at Basra from England on the 30th.

        Kut al Amara surrendered on the 29th. Captains S.C. Winfield-Smith, T.R.Wills, R.D.Corbett, S.C.B.Munday and Lieutenant C.H.C.Munro were made prisoners.

        Artillery ranging and general reconnaissance was carried out as usual during the month but was limited owing to food dropping expeditions.

209/22/13.
        On the first of May the squadron in the field comprised of :-

        6 B.E.2c's   (3 B.E.2c pilots).
        3 Maurice Farmans 3 Maurice Farman pilots not
        (Unserviceable) available for other machines.

209/22/12.
        "A" and "B" Flights moved from Camp Wadi to Shaikh Saad on the 6th.

        Captain Murray on a B.E.2c with Captain Thomson Glover as observer was attacked by a Fokker on the 8th whilst on reconnaissance east of Said Hashim. After having fired one and a half drums of Lewis Captain Murray was forced to land at Camp Wadi, a bullet having penetrated the petrol service tank.

        A reconnaissance on the 19th reported that the enemy had withdrawn from his advanced positions at Es Sinn and had concentrated at Shumran.

11.

The excessive heat now began to affect the personnel. Major Massy reports that:-

"From eight pilots in April the squadron flights in "the field suddenly dwindled to two pilots and finally to one "pilot each. All the others went to hospital more or less "knocked up directly after the strain, due to the feeding of "Kut, was over. The hot weather came on apace and there were "many admissions to hospital among the rank and file."

After the fall of Kut al Amara the following letter was addressed to the G.O.C. Tigris Corps from The Chief of the General Staff, Headquarters, I.E.F."D".

"The Army Commander desires you to convey to the "combined Air Service - The Royal Naval Air Service and the "Royal Flying Corps - his appreciation of their persistent "and meritorious work during the last few weeks.

"They have been called upon for very arduous and "trying efforts in keeping up the reconnaissance and "observation services, at the same time as the transport "of supplies to the beleaguered garrison of Kut.

"All this involved a very serious strain on all "ranks; but every call for their services was at once "responded to with readiness and resource."

Captain E.M.Murray assumed command of No.30 Squadron vice Major S.D.Massy with effect from 30.5.1916.

June 1916.

On the first of June, 1916, the Royal Flying Corps had the following aircraft in Mesopotamia :-

209/24/18.
209/22/13.

B.E.2c's	(Serviceable)	13
	(Repairable)	4
Maurice Farman	(Serviceable)	3
Shorthorns	(Repairable)	4

During the month the whole of the enemy's line was kept under continual observation by daily reconnaissances by "A" and "B" Flights including reconnaissances down the river Shatt el Hai as far as Kut el Hai of which photographs were taken. Bombs were dropped on Arab encampments at Gussabs Fort by two machines.

On the 27th pamphlets were dropped on Kut el Hai, informing the Arabs of the Declaration of War on the Turks by the Sharif of Mecca.

Meanwhile "C" Flight which was still at Basra received instructions to carry out a reconnaissance with two machines to Safwan to report on the encampment of Ibn Rashid. For this purpose an advanced landing ground was prepared at Zobeir on the 10th. The reconnaissance was accomplished on the 12th by two Maurice Farmans and photographs taken.

An enemy encampment was also observed at Jebel Sinam. For further reconnaissances to this place an advanced landing ground was established at Barjisiyah some sixteen miles south of Basra.

The R.N.A.S. Squadron left Mesopotamia on June 20th handing over to the Royal Flying Corps two Voisin Biplanes with spares.

12.

The personnel of No.30 Squadron was reinforced by the arrival at Basra during the month of 4 Flying Officers, 1 Observation Officer, and 77 Other Ranks.

July 1916.
209/24/19.

The state of aircraft in Mesopotamia on the 1st July, 1916 was:-

209/22/13.

	Serviceable.	Repairable.
B.E.2c's.	12	5
Maurice Farman Shorthorns	2	5
Voisins.	2	1

On the 4th "A" and "B" Flights of No.30 Squadron consisted of 8 B.E.2c's and 8 Pilots, of the aeroplanes three only were fit to take the air.

The average work of the squadron was one reconnaissance daily, and the area reconnoitred Shaikh Saad - Sannaiyat - Niadug-Kut-al-Amara - Kut al Hai - Gussabs Fort - Shaikh Saad. The reconnaissances up the Tigris towards the enemy's aerodrome at Shumran were made by two armed machines and by one machine when away from Shumran and towards Kut al Hai.

Seven pilot officers arrived at Basra on the 9th bringing the total pilots on the strength of the squadron to 19. The establishment of the squadron was now raised from 12 to 18 machines.

On the 11th a notable reconnaissance was made to Mandali, a distance of 95 miles, entailing a 3½ hour flight. Although a spare petrol tank was used only 5 pints of oil were left on the conclusion of the flight.

On the 12th two machines co-operated in driving off a hostile cavalry raiding party six miles south of Shaikh Saad, bombing the village in which they had sheltered.

"C" Flight with 3 pilot officers and 2 Voisin biplanes joined the squadron on the 17th.

With effect from this date the squadron came under the administration of the Middle East Brigade which was then forming in Egypt.

Major J.E. Tennant arrived at Basra on the 31st and assumed the command of No.30 Squadron.

During the month three types of enemy aeroplanes had been observed:-

1 Aviatik, 1 Fokker and 1 Morane.

August 1916.
209/22/15.
209/24/3.

At the beginning of August, 1916, the Squadron Depot was located at Amara and the Field base still at Shaikh Saad.

209/24/20.

An enemy Fokker attacked three B.E.2c's over Kut el Amara on the 13th, wounding Lieutenant J.H.B.Rodney before being driven down by machine gun fire by Lieutenant T.E.Lander and Lieutenant E.D. Barr, to land just within its own lines. The machine was immediately destroyed by our artillery fire.

"C" Flight proceeded to Arab Village on the 14th for attachment to the Headquarters of the 7th Division.

On the 14th/15th the first night-bombing raid was carried out on the Turkish aerodrome at Shumran by three B.E.2c's piloted by Captain H. de Havilland, Major J.E.Tennant and Captain J.H. Herring, sixteen 20 lb. and two 100 lb. bombs were dropped. The machines met with intense and concentrated rifle fire, but all returned safely.

Information having been received that a camp of 300 hostile mounted men was situated at Sahil, four machines set out on the morning of the 26th to bomb and attack this camp with machine gun fire. Twelve 20 lb. bombs were dropped from a height of 2,000 - 3,000 ft. The first four bombs were short but attracted people from the shelters and the next four were dropped on the crowd which had collected and amongst the shelters - they appeared to do a considerable amount of damage. The remaining four were dropped on the shelters further east. The machines then came down and opened machine gun fire on the various groups of shelters. 850 rounds were fired and though few people were seen to have been hit the effect should have been considerable as the bullets were seen striking right in the midst of the shelters. All machines returned safely.

Aziziya was reconnoitred by two machines on the 29th.

During the month artillery observation was carried out almost daily for the 7th and 14th Divisions and numerous small bombing raids undertaken in addition to general and photographic reconnaissances.

September 1916.
209/24/21.
209/22/16.

During September reconnaissances were carried out daily, the furthest being to Mandali, a distance of 95 miles. A total of 51 being made and 441 photographs taken.

Eight bombing raids were carried out of which six were on the enemy's aerodrome at Shumran on which seventy-eight 20 lb., two 100 lb. and four 112 lb. bombs were dropped. On the 23rd Lieutenant the Hon. J.H.B.Rodney descended to 100 feet to drop his bombs and Lieutenant J.S.Windor descended to under 100 feet and dropped two 20 lb. bombs within 10 yards of an Albatros machine on the ground.

On the same day a wire was received by the G.O.C. 3rd (Indian) Army Corps from G.H.Q. I.E.F. "D".

"Please convey to the Royal Flying Corps Army Commander's appreciation of plucky work carried out this morning."

Artillery co-operation was carried out daily, On one occasion three enemy guns were destroyed by direct hits.

Six Martinsyde Scouts arrived for the squadron during the month.

October 1916.
209/22/17.
209/24/22.

During October two hundred and fifty-eight hours of flying were done. Seven bomb raids were carried out including one night raid on the aerodrome at Shumran. A total of one hundred and thirty-five 20 lb. and eighteen 100 lb. bombs being dropped. The enemy machines were invariably on the ground during the daily reconnaissances over their aerodrome, and only once during the month was one met in the air, which retired after an indecisive fight.

14.

Sixty-three reconnaissance flights were made and three hundred and forty-four photographs taken. The photographic flights were most essential. No accurate maps of the country surrounding the banks of the Tigris were available and the whole district had to be carefully photographed for the purpose of constructing such maps.

Co-operation with the artillery resulted in 36 O.K's and 5 direct hits.

On the 3rd October the G.O.C. of the 15th Division operating on the Euphrates front stated that an aeroplane would be of the greatest assistance to him. The Army Commander approved of two machines being permanently attached.

On the 15th a detachment of "B" Flight consisting of 2 Pilots, 2 Observers and 9 Other Ranks with two machines arrived at Nasiriya from Arab Village.

Pending their arrival Lieutenant Rodney flew from Basra to Nasiriya on the 6th and on the 8th bombed Shattra on the Shatt el Hai.

"B" Flight moved from Shaikh Saad to Arab Village on the 7th followed by Squadron Headquarters on the 9th and "A" Flight on the 29th.

The disposition of the Squadron was now:-

Squadron Base	Basra
Squadron Depot	Amara
Squadron Headquarters	Arab Village
"A" Flight)	" "
"B" ½ Flight)	
"B" ½ Flight	Nasiriya att. to 15th Division.
"C" Flight	Arab Village att. to 7th Division.

November 1916.
209/22/18.
209/24/23.

During November 290 hours of flying was accomplished. Five bombing raids were carried out on the enemy aerodrome at Shumran. Three 112 lb. five 100 lb., two 65 lb. and one hundred and seventy-seven 20 lb. bombs being dropped. On one occasion Captain de Havilland completely destroyed an enemy Albatros by a direct hit with a 20 lb. bomb.

There were eight combats in the air, all of which were indecisive.

Artillery co-operation resulted in twenty-five O.K's on enemy gun pits and three direct hits on enemy guns being registered.

Eight-hundred and seven photographs were taken as compared with three hundred and forty-four in the previous month owing to the arrival of a William Aero Camera.

Meanwhile the detachment on the Euphrates front had carried out four bombing raids on enemy camps in the vicinity of Alain and generally reconnoitred the Euphrates to Shatra.

During the month an Advanced Echelon of Aircraft Park was established at Amara. This consisted of two Assistant Equipment Officers, 12 Other Ranks and one 100 ft. barge fitted to hold six months supply of spares for the squadron. The squadron was to be fitted from this Echelon. The Aircraft Park at Basra keeping the Advanced Echelon supplied.

209/24/1.

At the end of November the squadron had the following machines on charge:-

- 13 B.E.2c's.
- 3 Martinsyde Scouts.
- 3 Henri Farmans.

December 1916.
21/23/892.
209/22/2.
209/24/24.

After a period of preparation lasting until the 13th December, 1916, General Sir F.S. Maude began a concentrated offensive on the Tigris with Kut al Amara as his immediate objective.

The orders given to the Royal Flying Corps by General Headquarters were to carry out reconnaissances to ascertain that there were no hostile reinforcements within thirty miles distance of Kut in the direction of Bedrah, Aziziya or Afaq and to prevent enemy aircraft reconnoitring our position either during or after the bombardment, machines were also to be detailed to co-operate with the artillery of both Corps.

In addition they were to keep the Army Commanders constantly informed as to the movement of enemy troops and to keep the artillery of the III Corps informed as to the progress made by its infantry and by the cavalry.

In order that the various units might be recognised in this mission, which was contact patrol, ground signals of white calico for the various formations had been devised. Infantry brigades and battalions were allotted numbers which were placed after the Brigade or battalion signal.

In accordance with the above the following instructions were issued by the Officer Commanding No.30 Squadron :-

1. "A" Flight to detail two Martinsydes to be ready to leave the ground at one moment's notice of the presence of hostile aircraft from 6.30 a.m. to dusk, and it was stated that :-

   Any hostile machine that has come over our lines must be prevented from getting back to Shumran.

2. "B" Flight to carry out the following reconnaissanc reconnaissances :-

   (A) Arab Village - Jessan - Bughaila.
   (B) 20 miles south of Bughaila to Gussabs Fort.
   (C) To search the country within 30 miles of Kut in the direction of Bedrah, Aziziya and Afaq.

3. "C" Flight to co-operate with the Artillery of the I and III Corps.

   The observers of all machines on gaining their height and coming down to the aerodrome to search to the northwards for any indication of Arabs.

A portion of G.H.Q. moved forward to Battle Headquarters at Sinn Banks on the 13th from which date all machines landed at an advanced aerodrome nearby, and were met by an officer to whom they gave reports. Information thus reached the Army Commander with the greatest possible speed.

On the 14th two bombing attacks were made on Shumran Bridge (a bridge of boats spanning the Tigris at Shumran) in order to destroy the Turks only efficient means of reinforcing his troops on the right bank from those on the left. One bomb struck the end pontoon but did not appear to do any material damage.

The British advance on this day made it necessary for the Turks to withdraw the bridge upstream. An attempt to do this was discovered by Captain Herring on the night of the 15th/16th. He immediately commenced to bomb causing the tug to slip its tow and the pontoons to drift downstream into the bank. The tug ran aground two or three times. Twice he returned to Arab Village for bombs. As a result of this continued bombing the tug accomplished nothing and on the following day the Turks were without communication between their forces. The bridge was not re-established until the 17th.

For this act Captain Herring was awarded the D.S.O.

On the 20th Lieutenant G. Merton, observer Lieutenant W.A. Forsyth engaged an enemy Albatros over Shumran Aerodrome at a range of 40 yards, killing the observer and wounding the pilot who crashed his machine on landing.

A bomb raid was made on Bughaila on the 21st by 7 B.E.2c's and 3 Martinsydes, sixty-six bombs ranging from 20 lbs. to 112 lbs. were dropped resulting in considerable damage to the river bank and town.

On the 24th Captain de Havilland in a Martinsyde Scout reconnoitred Baghdad. He reported no unusual activity on the part of the enemy and no massing of Turkish troops.

For the remainder of the month the usual reconnaissance and artillery work was carried out.

In all a total of 509 hours of flying was done during the month and four tons of bombs dropped.

Meanwhile the "B" Flight detachment with the 15th Division had been carrying out general reconnaissance work on the Euphrates front from Nasiriya to Kut-al-Hai.

January 1917.
209/22/20.
209/24/25.
21/6/87.

During January, 1917, a total of 490 hours flying was done; daily reconnaissance and artillery co-operation continued.

Seventeen machines carried out bomb raids by day and three by night. The total number of bombs dropped was - one 336 lb., three 112 lb., twenty-two 100 lb. and sixty 20 lb.

Hostile aircraft were more active. Twelve combats having taken place, most of which were on the enemy's side of the line. On two occasions our machine was forced to land damaged.

Two hundred and fifteen photographs were taken.

On the 2nd it was discovered that the Turkish aerodrome had removed to a position five miles north-west of Shumran.

January 1917.
On the 11th January Major Tennant was promoted Wing Commander with the temporary rank of Lieutenant-Colonel on appointment as Officer Commanding Royal Flying Corps in Mesopotamia, and Captain de Havilland was promoted to Squadron Commander with the temporary rank of Major whilst so employed.

15/40/145.
The foregoing promotions were made in connection with the re-organisation of the Royal Flying Corps in Mesopotamia, which was to come into force with effect from the 1st February, 1917. The appointment of Assistant Director of Aeronautics was abolished and Officer Commanding Royal Flying Corps instituted.

On this day a message from General Headquarters was dropped into the Turkish trenches in the bend of river north-east of Kut inviting surrender with assurance of good treatment.

On the 14th Lieutenant J.E. Lander co-operating with the cavalry retirement from Hai Town, was forced to land in hostile country due to engine trouble and broke the undercarriage of his machine. The G.O.C. Cavalry Division gave orders to burn the machine; engine, Lewis guns and fittings were saved, and the pilot and observer brought in by the cavalry.

A landing ground was established at Atab on the 13th to facilitate co-operation with the III Corps on the Shatt al Hai.

On the 20th Major de Havilland and Lieutenants J.B. Lloyd and Windsor flying Martinsyde Scouts bombed the citadel of Baghdad. Six 100 lb. bombs were dropped. Three hit the citadel, two failed to explode and one exploded very feebly. One hit the citadel wall and two fell amongst houses destroying many and causing panic. A complete reconnaissance of Baghdad, Diyala and Ctesiphon was made from which special maps were prepared by General Headquarters.

"C" Flight proceeded to Sinn Abtar on detached duty on the 27th.

Lieutenant Colonel J.E. Tennant assumed command of the Royal Flying Corps in Mesopotamia with effect from the 31st.

At the end of January the detached half flight were still at Nasiriya carrying out reconnaissance work for the 15th Division.

February 1917.
On the 1st February Lieutenant Burns, observer Lieutenant L. Beevor Potts whilst co-operating with the artillery shot down an enemy Fokker which crashed just behind the Turkish lines.

During the period 4th to 10th co-operation with the artillery was especially successful, seventy targets were registered, six active batteries silenced, two direct hits obtained on enemy pontoon bridge at a range of 9,800 yards and in a high wind, one enemy barge sunk, enemy pontoons sunk and damaged.

As a result of a very accurate and valuable reconnaissance by Lieutenant G. Merton on the 8th the following message was received from the Chief of the General Staff:

"I am directed by the Army Commander to express "his appreciation of the excellent air reconnaissance carried "out by Lieutenant G. Merton, M.C., R.A.F. on the "8th February, 1917, whereby the new system of Turkish "entrenchments spanning the extremity of the Dahra loop was "plotted with such accuracy that his trace was practically "coincident with the trace of these works subsequently "recorded by air photography".

A further appreciation was received on the 10th :

"Army Commander's best congratulations to 104th "Battery and Royal Flying Corps in their fine co-operation "and the formers brilliant shooting".

The enemy machines were less active during this period, only two having been brought into action and three indecisive combats fought.

15/40/145.
21/6/87.

On the 15th the British Forces attacked and cleared the Dahra bend capturing 1995 prisoners. The work of the Royal Flying Corps during the fighting was mainly artillery co-operation in which four machines were engaged throughout the day. In this connection the following telegram was sent from Brigadier-General Bright, B.G.R.A. III Corps to Lieutenant-Colonel Tennant on the 16th February, 1917 :

"Please accept yourself and convey to your squadron "warmest thanks of all artillery III Corps for constant and "invaluable co-operation which alone rendered possible close "support of infantry".

On the 18th Major de Havilland whilst on escort duty attacked an enemy Fokker which made off towards its aerodrome. Major de Havilland followed and fired a drum of Lewis into it, whereupon one wing flew off and the other folded back against the fuselage. The enemy machine, turning round and round, went down vertically to crash near its own aerodrome.

On 22nd/23rd a bridge was thrown across the Tigris at Shumran. The role assigned to No.30 Squadron was to prevent enemy machines from leaving the ground and thus locating the bridge. To effect this a continuous patrol was maintained throughout the 23rd by the only two serviceable Martinsydes. One enemy machine managed to elude the vigilance of the patrolling machines at 5.0 p.m. but by then the bridge had been completed and supporting troops were going across.

An assault on the Sannaiyat position had also been launched on the 22nd and in the ensuing fighting the main work of the squadron was observation of artillery fire, keeping down enemy fire while the bridge was in course of construction, and reporting the progress of our infantry.

On the 24th Lieutenant Lloyd landed at Advanced G.H.Q. after a reconnaissance of Sannaiyat and reported the enemy in full retreat towards Baghdad; all available machines then concentrated on bombing and machine-gunning the retreating enemy. Major de Havilland scoring twenty-two direct hits with bombs in one day.

Lieutenant A.R. Rattray was wounded by rifle fire.

15/40/145.
21/6/87.
226/15/1.

On the 25th February the squadron, less "C" Flight, and the Euphrates Detachment were at Arab Village. "C" Flight were still at Sinn Abtar but rejoined the squadron at Zeur on the 7th March.

The squadron advanced a distance of over 150 miles by land and lengthened the river communications by about 250 miles. Owing to the tortuous course of the river it was impossible for the squadron transport to keep pace with the advance but three light tenders and two fast motor boats succeeded with difficulty in maintaining the most essential supplies.

The Royal Flying Corps arrangements for moving forward with the advance were as follows :

At each step a machine selected a landing ground as near as possible to the point reached by the G.H.Q. ship. Hangars were left behind. Several mechanics accompanied the light tenders. Pilots and observers flew on ahead carrying their rations with them.

Communication was constantly maintained by air between G.H.Q. and forward formations and also between G.H.Q. and the gunboats. Aerial communication was also maintained between the Cavalry Division and the forward commanders and both were kept informed of the enemy's disposition and movements.

An early reconnaissance on the 25th February located the main body of Turks at Bughaila still in retreat.

Lieutenant-Colonel Tennant machine-gunned a tug towing sections of the enemy's pontoon bridge up river towards Bughaila which was then bombed by Major de Havilland, the tug parted tow with the bridge and the pontoons drifted downstream. Thence to the 11th March, the day on which Baghdad was captured, the squadron continued to harass the retreating enemy by machine-gunning and bombing, moving up with the advancing forces and operating successively from Arab Village (25th February), Shumran Aerodrome (26th February), Shaikh Jaad (2nd March), Aziziya (3rd March), Zeur (5th March).

March 1917.

A reconnaissance to Baghdad on the 2nd March revealed the enemy preparing a position on the Diyala river.

In order to check the enemy's evacuation of guns and stores from Baghdad to Samarra by the Baghdad railway, Second Lieutenant J.S.Windsor with Captain Cave Brown, R.E., and Second Lieutenant R.K. Morris with Captain Farley, R.E., in B.E.2c's set out on the 7th March with charges of dynamite to destroy the railway bridge at Sumaikcheh, thirty-five miles north of Baghdad. A landing was made within two hundred yards of the bridge, when the Royal Engineers officers decided that the charges were not sufficient to destroy the bridge which was constructed of reinforced concrete, and as a party of mounted hostile Arabs appeared from a village some eight hundred yards away and were galloping towards them, it was decided to abandon the project. On leaving the ground both pilots emptied their Lewis guns into the Arabs who scattered.

On the 8th March the squadron flew from Zeur to Bustan and on the following day "C" Flight proceeded to Bawi to work with the I Corps.

A further attempt to intercept enemy railway transport was made on the 9th by Major de Havilland who succeeded in making a direct hit on the station near Kazimain with a 65 lb., blowing the roof off the station and destroying a train. The aerodrome and troops at Baghdad were also bombed; a total of forty-seven bombs being dropped during the day.

On the night of the 10th/11th the enemy evacuated his positions on the right banks of the Tigris and Diyala rivers and at 5.45 a.m. on the 11th the leading troops of the British forces entered Baghdad. "A" and "B" Flights landed at the Baghdad aerodrome in the afternoon and were joined by "C" Flight from Bawi on the day following.

After retreating from Baghdad the enemy divided into three separate forces :

i. On the Tigris Front, north of Baghdad, an army consisting of three Divisions which had retired from Kut al Amara.

ii. On the Euphrates Front a detachment of 2,000 men near Ramadi.

iii. On the Khaniqin Front (Diyala river) the XIII Turkish Army Corps.

Owing to the very scattered dispositions of the enemy's forces and the long distances of these from Baghdad, varying from eighty miles to the west and north to 120 miles to the north-east, the General Staff had to rely mainly on No.30 Squadron to obtain quick and accurate information regarding the movements and dispositions of the enemy.

In consequence, long distance flights were carried out daily over a new country with very inaccurate maps; pilots frequently having to work with maps of which the scale was 1/200,000.

In order to ensure that close co-operation was maintained with our advance troops and that their commanders received the earliest possible information of hostile movements, flights of the squadron were allocated as follows:

On the 26th "B" Flight was detached, together with a workshop barge, up the Diyala river to Baquba (thirty-five miles north-east of Baghdad) to work directly under the order of General Sir H.D'U.Keary's column which was operating against the Turks in the direction of Khaniqin.

On the 29th "C" Flight was sent up the Tigris to Kasirin to work directly under the orders of the III Corps.

"A" Flight (Martinsyde Scouts) and Squadron Headquarters remained at Baghdad for work on the Euphrates front and to carry out long distance reconnaissances under the instructions of General Headquarters.

The detachment at Nasiriya was recalled.

As the squadron at Baghdad was now 500 miles from its base at Basra, the Advanced Park at Amara was ordered to move to Shaikh Saad, about halfway between Basra and Baghdad.

During the month daily reconnaissances were made over the whole of the enemy's positions as far as Hit (Euphrates Front), Samara (Tigris Front) and Khaniqin (Diyala Front).

On the 22nd Lieutenant J.E.Lander, under instructions from G.H.Q. reconnoitred Khaniqin and the vicinity of Qasr-i-Shirin in an unsuccessful endeavour to locate the Russian Forces who were expected by about the 24th.

Another attempt was made on the 30th by Major de Havilland who flew for four and a half hours into Persia, but no trace of the Russian force was found. News was received later that they were held up in the Pai Tak Pass, thirty-five miles east of Qasr-i-Shirin.

On the 31st a reconnaissance to Hit, some 100 miles from Baghdad, revealed no unusual movements.

Enemy aerial activity was negligible during the month. One combat only having taken place, the hostile plane on being fired at immediately made off and landed on the Baghdad aerodrome.

April 1917.

Lieutenant-Colonel Tennant flying for five and a half hours in a Martinsyde Scout on the 2nd April located the Russian cavalry at Miankul about twenty-four miles east of Qasr-i-Shirin. He landed and was welcomed with the utmost enthusiasm. Despatches from General Headquarters for General N.W. Baratoff were handed to the Russian officer in command.

On the 4th April orders were issued by the General Staff for further offensive operations on both banks of the Tigris. The column on the right bank was under the command of Major-General Sir V.B. Fane and that on the left bank under Lieutenant-General Sir W.R.Marshall.

A flight of No.30 Squadron was allotted to each column. "B" Flight was withdrawn from Baquba and joined General Fane's column at Fort Kermea on the 5th. "C" Flight at Kasirin was detailed to work with the column on the left bank under General Marshall.

Squadron Headquarters moved up river from Baghdad to Fort Kermea on the 7th and "C" Flight moved from Kasirin to Sindiya (Kuwar Reach).

22.

Whilst on reconnaissance on the 1st April Lieutenant L.M.S. Page, observer Lieutenant A.R.Rattray in a B.E.2c were attacked by a hostile machine over Balad. In the ensuing manoeuvring for position the wing tips of the two machines collided. The enemy machine righted itself and made off in a northerly direction. Lieutenant Page managed to land at Kasirin with damaged wing tips. The following extract from the German version was intercepted by our wireless :

"One of our Fokkers piloted by Captain Schutz rammed "a hostile plane in air combat and caused it to fall. Our "machine brought back a 'wing' torn off the enemy plane and "landed safely in our lines."

According to Tribal report Captain Schutz's machine was compelled to land in the desert and was burnt. This was subsequently confirmed by a patrol of General Fane's column who found the remains on the 14th.

The first Bristol Scout was received by the squadron on the 5th being brought by Major de Havilland who flew from Baghdad to Basra and back, a distance of 750 miles in eight and a quarter hours actual flying time.

Reconnaissances on the 7th found the Turks digging new trenches at Harbe about twenty miles south-east of Samarra; located new camps and gun positions in the vicinity of the Adhaim river and the XIII Turkish Army Corps was located at Qara Tepe some eighteen miles south of Kifri.

On the 10th and 12th bombing attacks were carried out on Samarra, a direct hit with a 65 lb. bomb was obtained on a hostile machine and several upon rolling stock in the station.

226/7/34.

On the 15th Captain C.O.Pickering, observer Lieutenant H.W. Craig, in a B.E.2c, left at daybreak on reconnaissance duty and failed to return. Later, information was received that the machine had crashed after a fight with a hostile machine - both pilot and observer being killed.

On the 16th General Fane's column came under the command of General Sir A.S. Cobbe and on the 21st an attack was made on Istabulat.

During the preparation for and in the attack No.30 Squadron co-operated successfully with the forces employed; twelve reconnaissances and ten patrols being made. Artillery co-operation was carried out daily except on the 16th when weather prevented flying.

On the 18th April eleven targets were successfully ranged and the following telegram from B.G.R.A. III Corps was received by the O.C., R.F.C. :

"Many thanks for most invaluable co-operation today. AAA Three successive planes all put in excellent work."

"C" Flight moved to Barura on 19th followed by "B" Flight the next day.

On the 22nd Lieutenant M.L.Maguire on a Bristol Scout that he had flown up from Basra on the 17th, encountered a hostile Halberstadt over Istabulat, which he promptly shot to pieces in the air. The two port wings falling off before the machine crashed to earth from a height of 4,000 feet. This officer failed to return from a patrol on the 28th and information was subsequently received that he was wounded and a prisoner, having been shot down in combat by Captain Schutz.

Samarra station was captured on the 23rd and on the 26th preparations were made to bridge the Tigris and to occupy Samarra. General Marshall's column after crossing the river Adhaim on the 21st proceeded up river driving the enemy before them. On the 27th the enemy were found to have taken up a position at Bandi Adhaim,

During these operations the squadron co-operated consistently with both columns landing and reporting to column commanders. Thirteen reconnaissances were carried out but owing to the enemy continually withdrawing out of range only two artillery co-operation flights took place.

Aeroplane reconnaissance was now mainly confined to early morning and evening, on account of the intense heat during the day.

During the last two months, due to continual movements of the flights it was found quite impracticable to put the machines under hangars, and in order to protect them from the sun they were covered with Chattai matting (Palm leaf).

May 1917.
226/15/5.

The first few days of May saw the completion of the dispersal of the XIII Turkish Army Corps into the Jebel Hamrin and of the main defensive measures about Samarra.

The XVIII Turkish Army Corps were entrenching near Tekrit and the XIII Turkish Army Corps were retreating from Band-i-Adhaim towards Qara Tepe and quietness prevailed on the Euphrates Front. The British forces were able to withdraw to a defensive line to make preparations against the hot weather already well advanced.

"B" and "C" Flights were withdrawn from Barura on the 4th. Major de Havilland with three B.E.2c's of "B" Flight returned to Baghdad for reconnaissance of the Euphrates line and "C" Flight with six B.E.2c's and one Bristol Scout took up quarters at Sindiya for general reconnaissance work on the Tigris and Persian fronts.

The opportunity was now taken to thoroughly overhaul all machines of "A" and "B" Flights in the workshops of Baghdad.

On the 2nd May four B.E.2c's and two Martinsyde Scouts led by Major de Havilland bombed camps, columns and material of the XIII Turkish Army Corps at Adhaim, causing considerable damage and panic. Fourteen O.K's were obtained on targets and thirty-two bombs were all near enough to their objectives to be effective. Nearly half a ton of bombs was dropped.

Lieutenant Lander whilst on escort duty to a B.E.2c carrying out a reconnaissance over Tekrit on the 6th, encountered an enemy Halberstadt and after giving combat he was forced to land wounded behind the enemy lines where he was made prisoner.

During the month an extensive programme of photography of hostile country was commenced, for the compilation of maps and the correction of flood maps. It was expected that weather permitting this would take about three months.

The lull in the military operations now made regular Courses of Instructions for Pilots and Observers possible. These courses included lectures by artillery officers and also lectures and practical tests in every subject as dealt with by the latest pamphlets from France.

An elaborate mud model of the Istabult position with electric light fittings for gun flashes was constructed in the R.F.C. billet. The observer signalled from the roof and there were telephone receivers for the rest of the class in a gallery overlooking the model.

June 1917.

During the month of June the usual reconnaissance work was carried out on the three fronts. The programme of photography continued, 771 plates having been exposed. Much flying time was devoted to practising co-operation with the artillery and pilots of the B.E.2c's were given instruction in flying scouting machines.

No hostile aircraft were encountered. On various occasions enemy machines were seen on two of our fronts and over the Russians. Their methods were as a rule to send out one or two reconnaissance machines escorted by a Halberstadt, all flying very high. Their machines were reported to have been photographing the Russian front over Kizil Robat, Khaniqin and Qasir-i-Shirin.

Owing to the difficulty of transporting supplies consequent upon the fall of the Tigris, "C" Flight were withdrawn from Sindiya to Khan Jadida about the 23rd June, a point some twenty miles further downstream and midway between Baghdad and Sindiya.

On the 22nd Captain L.J.Bayly and Second Lieutenant A.E.L.Skinner on Martinsyde Scouts carrying eight 65 lb. bombs attacked a Turkish ship aground on the Tigris about ten miles north of Tekrit. One bomb exploded in the after part of the ship and another blew in her side. A direct hit was also obtained on a small dump ashore.

Four B.E.2c's bombed the camp of the XIII Turkish Army Corps south of Tekrit on the 27th. Twenty-two 20 lb. bombs were dropped. Seven direct hits were obtained on tents and infantry and nine others fell within a radius of twenty yards of tents etc.

The Army Commander (Lieutenant-General Sir F.S.Maude) was flown from Baghdad to Samarra by Lieutenant-Colonel Tennant on the 28th, to visit the advanced troops. The machine flying the Army Commander's flag was escorted by two others. Owing to delay the return journey was made by moonlight.

Three B.E.2c's of "B" Flight proceeded to Khan Jadida on detachment this day in relief of "C" Flight.

July 1917.

An Arab encampment in the neighbourhood of Imam Askar, about twenty-five miles east of Baquba, was bombed on the 3rd July by two machines, a Martinsyde Scout and a B.E.2c carrying four 65 lb. and eight 20 lb. bombs. Ten direct hits were obtained on tents and five drums of Lewis were fired into the scattered Arabs.

On the 10th two German aviators walked into Samarra and surrendered. Their machine - an Albatros - had forced landed in the desert through engine trouble on the day previous and had been burnt. They stated that another Albatros had forced landed and had also been burnt but that the pilot and observer had been unable to reach Samarra through sickness. An exhaustive search by armoured cars, cavalry and aeroplanes failed to locate the missing airmen.

In the operations against Ramadi on the 11th, four B.E.2c's co-operated with the military forces. One machine was employed on bombing, obtaining two direct hits with 20 lb. bombs on infantry and an ammunition wagon. Two machines co-operated with the artillery, registering two O.K's and the fourth was engaged on reconnaissance of the enemy position and movements. Messages and a sketch of the enemy position was dropped on the Headquarters of the VII Brigade. Two Martinsyde Scouts and a B.E.2c also endeavoured to leave their aerodrome at Baghdad to co-operate in the bombing but were driven down by the intense heat. The official shade temperature reaching 121 degrees.

During the month the Advanced Aircraft Park was moved up from Shaikh Saad to Baghdad.

August 1917.
226/5/45.

Early in August it was decided that Baquba would be the most suitable place for No.30 Squadron and on the 6th "C" Flight proceeded there from Baghdad. Later, on the 9th, "B" Flight was withdrawn from Khan Jadida to Baghdad pending the arrival of No.63 Squadron which was en route, and ultimately arrived at Basra on the 13th.

At the request of the Chief Political Officer, Rahalie, a village on the grain and trade route between Kerbela and the Turks at Hit was bombed on the 18th August by three Martinsyde Scouts and two B.E.2c's led by Captain L.J. Bayly. Five 65 lb. and twenty-eight bombs were dropped. Five direct hits were obtained, twelve bombs fell from 3-20 yards within their objectives and twelve failed to explode. The effect was to immediately bring the Shaikhs to submission.

On the 20th two machines co-operated in the capture of Sharaban. Several artillery ranging flights, contact patrols and reconnaissances were made.

Fort Hamrin, some seven miles north-east of Sharaban was bombed by two Martinsydes on the 22nd. Twelve 20 lb. and two 100 lb. bombs were carried. Direct hits were obtained on groups on infantry and cavalry and massed troops behind a hill were effectively machine-gunned.

A Turkish stronghold in Diwaniyeh on the Euphrates was bombed by Lieutenant B.E.Berrington on the 27th. For bombs the pilots used four converted 4.5 Howitzer H.E. shells fitted with forty second time fuses. These shells were dropped from heights of 5 feet, 20 feet, 30 feet and 2,000 feet. Two failed to explode and although no personal injuries were sustained by the garrison by the explosions from the other two, they surrendered to the Assistant Political Officer, fearing a repetition of the raid.

On the 29th a B.E.2e and B.E.2c were attacked by a hostile Albatros whilst on reconnaissance over the Jebel Hamrin range. Lieutenant Page in the B.E.2c succeeded in shooting in half the right hand main strut of the H.A. which thereupon made off.

The intense heat prevailing during the month seriously handicapped efforts at photography. For days together Martinsydes were unable to leave the aerodrome and frequently, when flown during a comparative lull in the heat, pilots returned worn out with the heavy strain of flying in an unduly high temperature. In spite of these adverse conditions 258 plates were exposed.

September 1917.
209/25/1.

The main work of the squadron for the first three weeks of September was photography. 742 films and 200 plates were exposed during the month covering an area of 400 square miles. The enemy's positions at Ramadi, Deli Abbas Durr, Bandi-i-Adhaim and the Jebel Hamrin area were photographed in detail. Revised maps of the Turkish positions on the Tigris and Diyala were prepared from the photographs and issued to the Army Commanders concerned. Photographs of the Ramadi position were issued to General Brooking's Column prior to the attack on the 29th.

On the 13th Major de Havilland, Squadron Headquarters and "A" Flight moved from Baghdad to Baquba and on the 21st "B" Flight complete with a photographic section moved from Baghdad to Falluja proceeding a further fifteen miles up river to Madhij on the 26th, to work with the 15th Division in the operations against Ramadi which opened on the 28th.

A photographic reconnaissance of Ramadi and Mushaid had been carried out on the 27th and 18 photographs taken. On the 28th four machines made an early reconnaissance of Ramadi and Hit reporting no unusual enemy activity. During the day one machine carried out contact patrol, one artillery co-operation and one patrol of the Ramadi area. No enemy aircraft were encountered. Captain Merton was wounded in both knees by M.G. fire from the ground. On the following day three machines co-operated with the artillery and one was engaged in general reconnaissance.

The operations terminated on the 29th by the unconditional surrender of the Turkish garrison.

209/25/2.

"B" Flight returned to Falluja on the 3rd October.

209/18/7.

On the 12th Lieutenant Page in a B.E.2c whilst on escort duty to a machine on reconnaissance had a forced landing in hostile country near Nahrin Kopri owing to a cracked cylinder. Lieutenants P.F. West and F.G.O. Dickinson in a B.E.2e landed, picked up Lieutenant Page and got off again just as some mounted Arabs appeared.

A demonstration was carried out by two machines on the 13th over Kerbela, fifty miles south-west of Baghdad. One machine forced landed near the town. The occupants were treated in a friendly fashion by the Arabs; some of whom craved for a joy ride.

A successful bombing raid on three Arab camps a few miles south-west of Baghdad was carried out on the 25th. The shelters and tents were totally destroyed with 20 lb. bombs, and machine-gun fire from a height of 300-500 feet caused many casualties.

209/25/1.

Two machines were temporarily detached from Baquba on the 27th to work with a column under Brigadier-General C.E.G. Norton whose objective was Mandali. Working from a landing ground at Baled Ruz. On the 29th reconnaissances of the Mandali - Kazaniya road and Khaniqin - Mandali road were carried out. No enemy movement was seen. Messages were dropped on the main body of General Norton's column. Mandali was occupied this day and the two machines rejoined the squadron in the evening.

The squadron received its first Spads during the month, one arriving at Baghdad on the 15th and the other on the 17th.

October 1917.

At the beginning of October, 1917, the location of the squadron was as follows :

Headquarters "A" and "C" Flights - Baquba.
"B" Flight - Madhij (to Falluja 3.10.17).

On the 5th October three B.E.2c's of "B" Flight bombed a supposed ammunition dump at Hit. Sixteen 20 lb. bombs were dropped but no explosions were observed.

Owing to increased hostile aerial activity the enemy aerodrome at Kifri was bombed on the 16th by three Martinsydes from Baquba. Six 112 lb. and twelve 20 lb. bombs were dropped. Two of the 112 lb. bombs fell within ten yards of machines on the ground. Our machines were met with machine-gun fire from the ground. One machine had the main tank pierced and on the return journey was forced to land fifteen miles outside Kifri. The machine was burnt and the pilot picked up by one of the other Martinsydes.

On the 18th Headquarters and "C" Flight moved from Baquba to Sharaban to co-operate with the III Corps against the Turks at Deli Abbas. The following day reconnaissances were made of the Kifri - Qara Tepe area. In the attack one machine was engaged on contact patrol with the 14th Division; three machines in artillery co-operation and one on contact patrol with the cavalry. On the 25th one machine ranged two enemy guns and ten O.K's. were obtained. Headquarters and "C" Flight returned to Baquba that evening.

On the 24th Lieutenant P.F. West dropped eight 20 lb. bombs on camps in the Jebel Hamrin and on the same day six machines set out to bomb a party of hostile Persian gendarmerie reported 800-2000 strong marching towards Kifri from the east. These could not be located and no bombs were dropped in consequence. On the 31st three Martinsydes and three B.E.2c's again set out on the same errand. One of the B.E's. forced landed at Sharaban. The other five failing to locate the hostile gendarmerie bombed Kifri aerodrome. Lieutenant A.P. Adams had the petrol tank of his B.E. pierced in several places and forced landed near Narim Char. He destroyed his machine and was picked up by Lieutenant F.Nuttall in a Martinsyde. Lieutenant Welman in a Martinsyde was shot down and landed at Kifri and was made prisoner.
Lieutenant C. Cox in a Martinsyde had his radiator pierced by a piece of shell and was forced to land ten miles N.E. of Qizil - Ribat. He burned his machine and walked into our lines, covering a distance of eighteen miles in 6½ hours.

Meanwhile "B" Flight on the Euphrates front carried out several reconnaissances of the Hit area.

Several indecisive combats took place during the month. Photographic activity resulted in 872 plates and films being exposed covering an area of 327 square miles.

November 1917.
209/25/4.
15/229/2.

During November there were no active operations on the Diyala and Euphrates fronts and the work of the squadron consisted of occasional reconnaissances of the Jebel Hamrin and Hit areas, bombing raids and hostile aircraft patrols combined with an extensive programme of photography. On the Diyala front 880 exposures were made and 201 on the Euphrates front. On the latter front heavy rain and low clouds greatly hampered this work.

On the 8th November enemy camps at Qara Tepe and Nahrin Kopri (Jebel Hamrin area) were bombed by three machines from Baquba (B.E.2c, B.E.2e and R.E.8). Twenty-two 20 lb. bombs and two boxes of darts were dropped from 5000-6000 feet. Mud huts were destroyed, troops scattered and many casualties caused. Two days later these camps were again bombed by five machines. Five 112 lb., twenty-four 20 lb. bombs and two boxes of darts were dropped and camps heavily machine-gunned. Huts and tents were demolished and many casualties caused to personnel and animals.

On the 24th "B" Flight carried out a demonstration flight over Kufa, Abu Sakanr and Nejef on the lower Euphrates for the benefit of Arabs of doubtful tendencies.

The squadron had four indecisive combats during the month.

December 1917.
209/18/2.
209/25/6.
15/229/2.

On the 2nd December Headquarters "A" and "C" Flights of No.30 Squadron moved up the Diyala from Baquba to Qala Mufti to co-operate with the III Corps in the operations against the enemy in the direction of Qara Tepe. These flights had been reinforced by two machines from "B" Flight.

In order to prevent enemy aerial reconnaissance prior to the attack, the aerodrome at Kifri was bombed by two machines on the night of the 30th November/1st December. Sixteen 20 lb. bombs were dropped, of which six failed to explode. It was thought that the machines on the ground were hit by splinters.

The attack was opened on the 3rd and by the 6th Nahrin Kopri had been taken and our troops occupied positions at Qizil Ribat and the Sakaltutan Pass and on this day the pursuit of the Turks who were retreating towards Kifri was discontinued.

During the operations the work of No.30 Squadron consisted mainly of reconnaissances, contact patrols and harassing the retreating enemy with machine-gun fire. Little artillery co-operation was possible due to the rapid retirement of the enemy. Nahrin Kopri was occupied on the 4th, machines were engaged throughout the day on artillery observation, contact patrol and reconnaissance work with the cavalry and III Corps. The retreating enemy were heavily machine-gunned.

On the 5th four enemy guns were prevented from coming into action by Lieutenant A.W. Hawkins (pilot) and Lieutenant A.H. Lindop (observer) who machine-gunned the teams from a low altitude, scattering and killing many of the horses.

During the whole of the operations enemy aircraft were inactive. On one occasion an enemy Albatros took off from the Kifri aerodrome but made no endeavour to climb or attack our machines.

On the 8th a general reconnaissance of the Kifri area revealed no sign of enemy movement. On this day Headquarters, "A" and "C" Flights returned to Baquba.

Until the end of the month machines kept up a general observation of the Kifri area.

An enemy aerodrome established at Tuz Khurmatli was bombed by three R.E.8's of No.30 Squadron on the 19th, two with eight 20 lb. bombs each and the third with a 112 lb. and two 20 lb. bombs. One 20 lb. bomb fell within ten yards of a machine and the 112 lb. bomb within fifty yards. Three enemy machines rose from the ground. One was driven down, the second circled round underneath the bombers and the third followed the formation back to the Jebel Hamrin but did not attack.

On the 28th Humr aerodrome was bombed by eleven machines of No.63 Squadron assisted by three R.E.8's of No.30 Squadron. Four enemy aircraft were observed on the ground. Over a ton of bombs were dropped. At one particular moment eleven bombs were seen to burst simultaneously around and among the E.A's. Pilots and observers agreed that the machines must have been destroyed. One hangar was left in flames.

On the 30th three E.A. were observed on the old aerodrome at Kifri. These were bombed by four machines of No.63 Squadron and five of No.30 Squadron. The former squadron dropped two 112 lb. and sixteen 20 lb. bombs and the latter thirty-four 20 lb. bombs. Bombs fell within 30-100 yards of the machines.

209/18/2.

The following interesting document was captured on the Diyala front during the operations :

"To the Commandant of the 156th Regiment.

1. "In order to deceive the aeroplanes from the time "that they are in sight, the infantry battalions which are at "Karatapa along with the 1st Battalion of the 156th Regiment "which is at the south of Narin, will at once take the road "towards Jabal Himrin without waiting for an order, without "striking the tents or taking their packs.

"They will contonue their march until the "aeroplanes have disappeared and will rest at the place at "which they will arrive. If the aeroplanes are returning, "the battalions will continue their march towards Jabal "Himrin, until they are no longer in sight and then will "return to their own camp.

2. "The gunners along with the machine-guns will fire at the aeroplane without waiting for an order.

        Acting Commander of the 6th Division.
        Kaynimre Kain
        Mihamad Amin."

Photography on the Diyala front during the month of December resulted in the exposure of 201 plates.

There were no active operations on the Euphrates front. "B" Flight carried out the usual reconnaissance work. Several demonstration flights were made over hostile Arab tribes in the vicinity of Hilla, Kerbela and Nejef. 163 photographs were taken during the month.

On the 22nd December the squadron received its first D.H.4 which was flown from Basra to Baghdad by Captain F. Nuttall in four hours five minutes. This was the first non-stop flight made between these two places.

January 1918.

209/25/26.
207/72.
15/229/2.
209/18/16.

No active military operations were undertaken during the month. The squadron being employed in the usual reconnaissances, photography and bombing raids. 125 plates were exposed on the Diyala front and 151 on the Euphrates. On two occasions only were E.A. encountered over our lines. On the 21st an Albatros C.III forced landed near Felluja with a small end seized. The occupants were able to burn their machine before capture. On the 31st an E.A. was shot down by Lieutenants A.E.L.Skinner and R.K.Morris in Spads, and landed in the vicinity of Qala Mufti. The machine was burnt and the pilot and observer succeeded in effecting their escape.

On the 2nd an expedition set out for Karind with the object of bringing in Colonel Kennion, H.B.M. Consul at Kermanshah, a British Wireless Section which had been operating with the Russians, and a Survey Party. One machine went out on the 3rd to assist the column in any way possible. A reconnaissance of the Qala Shirwin area revealed no opposition for ten or fifteen miles; a message to this effect was dropped on the column. On its return the column occupied Qasr-i-Shirin where a landing ground and petrol dump was established as a refilling point for machines proceeding to Kermanshah.

On the 3rd three machines of No.30 Squadron co-operated with nine machines of No.60 Squadron in bombing Humr aerodrome. Seventy-two 20 lb. and seven 112 lb. bombs were dropped. Owing to clouds the effect of the raid was uncertain.

On the 17th Lieutenants A.S. Mills and W.Taylor were reported missing in an R.E.8, having failed to return from a reconnaissance to Haditha, a distance of eighty miles up the Euphrates from Ramadi. It was subsequently learnt that they were forced to land with engine trouble and after burning their machine and walking thirty miles they were eventually captured by a Turkish patrol.

A demonstration was carried out against Qala Shirwin and the neighbouring villages on the 20th by one howitzer battery and seven aeroplanes. This vicinity being the centre of activity of the Turkish and German Local Political Officers. The battery confined its attention to

Qala Shirwin while the machines bombed and machine-gunned Kellar and Sheikh Sa'ad Shakal. Forty bombs were dropped and 700 rounds of ammunition fired. Kellar was again bombed on the 22nd by two machines. Eight 20 lb. bombs were dropped and ten drums of ammunition fired into the village.

On the 21st six machines of No.30 Squadron escorted by two S.P.A.D's and in co-operation with six machines of No.63 Squadron carried out a raid on Kifri aerodrome. The formations met at 4,000 feet over the objective on which eight E.A. were drawn up. Two 112 lb. and seventy-seven 20 lb. bombs were dropped. No direct hits on E.A. were scored but several bursts were observed within ten yards of the machines.

During the raid a D.H.4 of No.30 Squadron was destroyed in the air by a direct hit from A.A. fire, and the pilot, Lieutenant W.S.Bean and observer, Lance-Sergeant R.G. Castor, were killed.

Lieutenants L.H. Browning and A.W.Hawkins in R.E.8's flew to Kermanshah on the 23rd returning the following day with despatches from Colonel Kennion. On this occasion the landing and refilling point at Qasr-i-Shirin was utilised.

Baghdad was bombed by two E.A. on the night of the 24th/25th. A few casualties were inflicted in a hospital but no material damage done. In retaliation Humr and Kifri aerodromes were bombed on the night of the 25th/26th by Nos. 63 and 30 Squadron respectively. Five flights were made to Kifri, the first starting at 8.30 p.m. and the last finishing at 6.35 a.m. Forty 20 lb. bombs were dropped and 1600 rounds of ammunition fired.

During this raid a D.H.4 piloted by Lieutenant Nuttall with Lieutenant R.R.B. Sievier as observer, was forced to land two miles N.E. of Qara Tepe behind the enemy lines. The engine had caught fire at 1,000 feet. After making a perfect landing and taking a Lewis gun apiece the machine was left to burn and the pilot and observer making a detour to avoid enemy patrols regained our lines the following morning after completing a distance of twenty-four miles.

Towards the end of January it became necessary to convey Colonel Stokes C.I.E. "I" Branch with all speed to the British Legation at Tehran. On the 25th Lieutenant Browning in an R.E.8 with Colonel Stokes as passenger and accompanied by Lieutenant Adams in another R.E.8 carrying oil and petrol set out for Kermanshah en route for Tehran. Landing at Qasr-i-Shirin to refuel, Lieutenant Browning unfortunately crashed his machine in taking off. Another machine was sent up and a successful start was made on the 26th. One arrival at Kermanshah Lieutenant Browning's machine was refuelled from the accompanying R.E.8 and was thus enabled to complete the further 300 miles to Tehran arriving there on the 28th.

On the 31st a reconnaissance of the Mandali - Nehkidir neighbourhood was carried out to ascertain the disposition of Arab encampments. The camp of Ali Shimal who had been causing trouble was located at the latter place and on the 1st February his camp was bombed and machine-gunned by Captain G.M.Smyth, five 20 lb. bombs were dropped.

February 1918.

As it was intended to resume operations on the Euphrates front later during the month, a demonstration was carried out on the 14th by two columns of the 13th and 14th Divisions in the direction of Qara Tepe with a view to mystifying the enemy as to our intentions. The 13th Division column from Sakaltutan Pass to Nahrin Kopri; the 14th Divisional column from Mirjana to Keshpul Qadeem. Both columns returned after dark without encountering enemy troops.

In conjunction with this demonstration ten machines flew over the enemy lines and bombed and machine-gunned any enemy or camps encountered. Fifty-six bombs were dropped and 3,600 rounds fired at ground targets.

On the 13th and 15th photographic reconnaissances of the area south-west of Qara Tepe were made and on the 14th a low flying reconnaissance to ascertain if enemy troops were moving or massing in areas south or south-east of Qara Tepe revealed no movements or massing.

On the 21st Uqbah on the Euphrates was occupied without casualties and shortly afterwards aerial reconnaissance reported that the enemy had evacuated his trenches south of Hit and had occupied a position on the Broad Wadi between Hit and Sahiliya. "B" Flight carried out general reconnaissance and contact patrol during these operations.

"B" Flight moved from Falluja to Ramadi on the 23rd where they were joined on that day by "A" Flight and two machines of "C" Flight from Baquba and "A" Flight of No.63 Squadron from Samarra. With these flights a composite squadron under the command of Major de Havilland was formed. This squadron carried out a vigorous offensive against the enemy. Troops and enemy aeroplanes at Hit were bombed and machine-gunned by day and night. One E.A. was destroyed by a direct hit with a 20 lb. bomb and others damaged, horse lines were hit and horses stampeded; leaders of a gun team were killed and the column disorganised; a machine-gun was silenced; camps and bivouacs were machine-gunned.

In addition to this offensive, detailed reconnaissances of the country between our outposts and Baghdadi were carried out. The movements of the enemy were fully reported and all important positions photographed. On the 26th, the aerial offensive was ordered to stop and the following day "A" Flight of No.63 Squadron returned to Samara.

Owing to the continuous bombing the enemy removed his aerodrome to Haditha, fifty miles back from Hit.

E.A. were fairly active during the month being reported over our lines on seventeen occasions and although several combats took place, no decisive results were obtained.

"C" Flight on the Diyala front carried out a reconnaissance in the vicinity of Khan-i-Chakal on the 24th to locate the German Political Officer, von Drueffel. He was unwise enough to open fire at the machine with a machine-gun thereby exposing his position. As a result of this reconnaissance four R.E.8's, two from No.83 Squadron and two from No.30 Squadron, set out on the 26th to bomb von Drueffel

One machine of each squadron reached the objective. Sixteen 20 lb. bombs were dropped, six signallers were killed but the political officer escaped.

March 1918.
209/25/28.
207/72.

On the 1st March Headquarters of No.30 Squadron moved from Baquba to Uqbah where they were joined on the 9th by "A" and "B" Flights from Ramadi.

On the 4th Captain L.F. Haight and Lieutenant H.L.W. Hancock failed to return from a low reconnaissance of the Hit - Baghdadi road. Two search reconnaissances on the following day located the machine which had been burnt, 2½ miles E.N.E. of Hit. It was subsequently learned that they had been brought down by rifle fire and made prisoners.

An aerial reconnaissance on the 8th reported that the enemy were evacuating Hit the occupation of which was immediately carried out by our troops.

On the evening of the 8th the retreating enemy were machine gunned and bombed by all available machines. Thirty-three 20 lb. bombs were dropped from low altitudes. Eleven O.K's were obtained, nine on camps and bivouacs, one on a camel troop and one on twenty-five cavalry; 1500 rounds of ammunition were fired, men and animals were seen to fall. The aerial offensive was continued on the following day when the enemy retreated as far as Sahiliya. One hundred and thirty nine 20 lb. and twenty-five 16 lb. bombs were dropped and 7,300 rounds of ammunition fired. Havoc was caused among troops and transport. Bombing on this day began at dawn and continued at short intervals until dusk.

On the night of the 9/10th the enemy retired from Sahiliya to their forward position at Khan Baghdadi twenty-two miles above Hit. Aeroplane reconnaissances kept the Army commanders fully posted as to the movements of the enemy throughout.

On the 10th 6 R.E.8's bombed and machine-gunned troops, transport and camps at Khan Baghdadi and in the vicinity of Sahiliya fifteen 25 lb. and thirty 20 lb. bombs were dropped. Eight O.K's. were obtained. Khan Baghdadi was again bombed on the 12th.

"A" and "B" Flights moved from Uqbah to Hit on the 11th.

On the 14th a reconnaissance to Ana revealed no enemy troops or camps.

Two flights of No.63 Squadron arrived at Hit from Samarra on the 25th.

Operations which resulted in the capture or destruction of the whole Turkish Force on the Euphrates Front commenced on the 26th. Cavalry and armoured cars left at 9.0 p.m. on the night of the 25th/26th, making a wide detour round the enemy's right flank. By the evening of the 26th they were astride the Khan Baghdadi-Haditha road in rear of the enemy, who had been expelled from his position by an Infantry attack in the morning. Cut off on all sides the enemy surrendered. The cavalry pressed on and occupied Ana on the 28th and the Armoured cars pursued the enemy to a point 73 miles beyond the Aleppo Road, rounding up many prisoners including a number of Germans.

34.

The composite squadron of two flights of No.30 Squadron and two flights of No.63 Squadron co-operated throughout the 26th and in addition to reconnaissance and artillery work, twenty-one machines dropped 3614 lbs. of bombs on suitable targets and used machine guns effectively.

Many casualties were inflicted and bodies of enemy dispersed. In conjunction with the ground operations on the 27th eleven machines continued to harass the enemy; 3014 lbs. of bombs were dropped and 1,300 rounds of S.A.A. fired. As a whole, targets were small and scattered but good results were obtained. A direct hit was obtained on a launch and another on an ammunition dump which was blown up. No E.A. were seen during the operations. One flight of No.63 Squadron returned to Samarra on the 28th.

On the Diyala Front three E.A. on Kifri aerodrome were bombed by an R.E.8 from "C" Flight at Baquba. Eight 20 lb. bombs were dropped and one E.A. was damaged.

On the 4th Lieutenant R.K. Morris in a S.P.A.D. whilst escorting an R.E.8 on reconnaissance was attacked by an Albatros. A short combat ensued when the E.A. broke off and disappeared into the clouds.

On the 11th Von Druefells house at Khan-i-Chakal was again bombed by two machines. Two 112 lb. and four 20 lb. bombs were dropped. No direct hits were obtained but more of his native signallers were reported to have been killed.

Three machines dropped twenty four 20 lb. bombs on Arab encampments near Mandali on the 21st and machine-gunned the inhabitants.

Photography was carried out in the Kifri area for mapping purposes on the 20th and 21st. Aspect photos of Von Drueffel's position were taken and prints distributed to the Political Officer in an endeavour to trace the German Political Officer's actual headquarters.

On the 25th a demonstration was made by the 13th and 14th Divisions on the Diyala Front with a view to distracting the enemy's attention from the Euphrates Front. Two machines from Baquba co-operated throughout, but met with no opposition.

Photography during the month resulted in 303 exposures on the Diyala front and 475 on the Euphrates front. E.A. were reported over our lines on fourteen occasions during the month. They were encountered three times and on each occasion the combat was indecisive.

April 1918.
209/25/29.
207/72.
21/6/87.

Headquarters and "A" Flight of No.30 Squadron returned to Baquba on the 5th April leaving "B" Flight still detached at Hit. "B" Flight had returned to Ramadi by the 14th and on the 15th sent a half flight of three machines to reinforce the squadron at Baquba.

During the first three days of the month great damage was caused by a violent storm which raged for three days. The storm reached it's height on the night of the 1/2nd. Two of No.63 Squadron's hangars at Samarra were demolished, totally wrecking two R.E.8's and damaging seven others. Another R.E.8 of No.30 Squadron was destroyed at Hit. This machine was blown over although it was held down by two men and three screw pickets on each wing.

On the Euphrates front no active operations were undertaken during the month, the work of the detached half flight consisting of general and photographic reconnaissances. Four hundred and eighty plates were exposed. No E.A. were encountered.

On the 7th a reconnaissance was sent to Abu Kemal, sixty miles beyond Ana to investigate a report that the enemy was bringing up reinforcements to Ana. A cavalry patrol only was seen.

No operations were undertaken on the Diyala front during the first three weeks of April. General and photographic reconnaissances were carried out. Sketching reconnaissances of various areas with a survey officer as passenger were carried out on the 11th and 12th to assist in speedy compilation of maps.

On the 11th a general reconnaissance of the Umr Maidan area was carried out, and the Tuz Khurmatli - Kifri area was reconnoitred on the 16th. Troops and tentage were reported upon but little change was noted. The distance flown was 175 miles.

Between the 7th and 13th 176 photographs were taken of the Kulawand - Kifri area.

On the 15th three R.E.8's from "B" Flight arrived at Baquba from Radami and on the 19th the squadron was further reinforced by "A" Flight of No.63 Squadron from Samarra with 6 machines. ("A" Flight of No.63 Squadron had taken 1 machine from "B" Flight and 1 from "C" Flight to bring it up to strength) Major de Havilland, D.S.O., left the squadron on the 21st on transfer to the Home Establishment and Major O.A. Westendarp assumed command of the squadron.

Military operations which aimed at enveloping and destroying the Turkish Forces in the Tuz Khurmatli-Kifri area commenced on the 24th. Four columns of troops were organized for these operations i.e. A, B, C and D. "B" was subdivided into B1 and B2. Aeroplanes were allotted as follows:-

Column A :-   "A" Flight of No.30 Squadron - six R.E.8's to carry out reconnaissances and co-operation.

Column B :-   (B1) "C" Flight of No.30 Squadron - three R.E.8's.
              (B2) "A" Flight of No.63 Squadron - three R.E.8's.

Both Flights to carry out reconnaissance on the third day of operations and contact patrol for both columns on the fourth day of operations.

Column C :-   "B" Flight of No.30 Squadron - three R.E.8's for reconnaissance and artillery co-operation.

Column D :-   "A" Flight of No.63 Squadron - three R.E.8's for reconnaissance and artillery co-operation.

"A" Flight of No.30 Squadron and "A" Flight of No.63 Squadron were in addition to be held in readiness to assist "C" Flight of No.30 Squadron in carrying out the work required by the main columns B.1 and B.2.

"C" Flight of No.72 Squadron at Mirjana was also placed under the orders of No.30 Squadron for these operations.

No.72 Squadron was formed at Upavon on the 2nd July, 1917 under the command of Major H.W.Von Poellnitz and arrived at Basra on the 2nd March, 1918.

During the few days preceding the 24th important reconnaissances were carried out of the enemy's positions and camps at Tuz-Khurmatli, Kulawand, Qara Tepe, Ain Faris and Abu Gharaib and the areas in these vicinities.

During the operations machines co-operated closely with the advancing columns, landing in the vicinity of Column Headquarters and conveying their information direct. Enemy troops and transport were vigorously and successfully bombed and machine gunned.

On the 26th three R.E.8's of No.30 Squadron and one of No.63 Squadron dropped twenty 25 lb. bombs on scattered bodies of troops on the Qara Tepe - Kifri road and on the following day retreating troops in the Tuz-Khurmatli area were bombed by five machines of No.30 Squadron. Twenty-three 25 lb. and twelve 20 lb. bombs were dropped and fourteen O.K's obtained. Three Bristols of No.72 Squadron on offensive patrol machine-gunned troops in the Kifri area. One machine of No.30 Squadron dropped eight 25 lb. bombs at Kulawand, obtaining O.K's on troops and horses.

ara Tepe, Abu Alik and Abu Gharraib were occupied on the 27th, Kifri on the 28th and Tuz Khurmatli on the 29th. An advanced aerodrome was established at Umr Maidan on the 27th.

Throughout the 28th aeroplanes again reconnoitred roads and trenches north-west of Tuz Khurmatli, bombing and machine-gunning enemy troops, transport and batteries. Six machines of No.30 Squadron carried out bombing and machine gun operations over Tuz Khurmatli, Yanija and the Tuz-Tauq road: thirty-three 25 lb. and eight 20 lb. bombs were dropped, six O.K's were obtained. 1,100 rounds were fired at ground targets with good effect. A further two machines of No.30 Squadron dropped sixteen 25 lb. bombs on enemy troops retreating to Tuz Khurmatli.

On the Persian border certain tribes, notably some sections of the Sinjabis, were inclined to be troublesome and as they were situated just north of the Qasr-i-Shirin - Kermanshah road it was deemed necessary to take punitive measures against them and acting in conjunction with a small column, two machines of No.72 Squadron machine-gunned villages and camps north-east of Abi-i-Zerish in the Sinjabis country on the 24th. The following day two machines of No.30 Squadron led by two of No.72 Squadron again machine-gunned and bombed these villages. Eleven 25 lb. bombs were dropped from 200 feet and six O.K's on tents obtained 950 rounds of ammunition fired at the inhabitants.

May 1918.
209/25/30.
21/6/87.
207/72.
15/229/2.

At the beginning of May orders were received from England that operations were to be continued with the object of capturing and holding Kirkuk. The troops were re-organised into Columns A and B and an additional force was formed to guard the lines of communication. Kirkuk being some 130 miles from our nearest railhead "C" Flight of No.30 Squadron was placed at the disposal of these columns and on the 2nd it proceeded to Tuz Khurmatli. The flight was by this time reduced to four machines. On the 4th "C" Flight of No.72 Squadron with four Bristol Scouts arrived at Tuz Khurmatli from Mirjana to provide escorts. The Squadron was now working under great difficulties some 80-100 miles from its base. To facilitate the suply of the Flight at Tuz an advanced dump was established at Chaman Kopri.

Reconnaissances of Taza Khurmatli were carried out on the 1st, 2nd and 4th and of Kirkuk and Altun Kopri on the 5th.

Enemy movements in the Kirkuk area and on the roads leading to Altun Kopri were kept under continuous observation. Camps in the vicinity of Arbil sixty miles North of Kirkuk were reported on.

Aeroplane reconnaissance on the 6th reported the evacuation of Taza Khurmatli which was occupied by our troops on this day.

On the 7th May our troops entered Kirkuk unopposed, the enemy having withdrawn during the night of the 6th/7th. The retiring enemy were machine-gunned and their disposition reported to Column A. Troops and cavalry five miles northeast of Kirkuk and transport on road to Alton Kopri were successfully attacked by machine-gun fire by a Bristol monoplane of "C" Flight of No.72 Squadron.

On the 12th five R.E.8's and one Martinsyde Scout of No.30 Squadron attacked Turkish camps in the vicinity of Arbil. Forty-five 25 lb. bombs were dropped and 10 O.K's registered. This raid was repeated on the 15th when six R.E.8's dropped thirty-nine 20 lb. bombs and fired six hundred rounds of S.A.A. from heights of 1000-5000 feet, nine O.K's were obtained. On the 17th thirty-two 20 lb. bombs were dropped on the Altun Kopri aerodrome by five R.E.8's of No.30 Squadron escorted by one Bristol Scout of No.72 Squadron, damaging two machines and one hangar.

In the raid of the 15th, on arrival at Altun Kopri sighting no E.A. on the aerodrome the formation divided to bomb and machine gun suitable targets, but the enemy had six Albatros Scouts concealed in a field some miles from the aerodrome. Three of these surprised and shot down in flames Lieutenants J.O.Alison and F.W.Atherton. Lieutenants L.H. Browning and F.C. Kirk shot down an E.A. which landed safely. The pilot attempted to run for cover but Lieutenant Browning, descending to 800 feet, released a 20 lb. bomb which fell within a yard from the running airman, completely obliterating him. Lieutenant M.W.Thomas of "C" Flight, No.72 Squadron, drove down another to land.

On the return flight Captain L.M.S.Page was attacked by two Albatros Scouts, one of which succeeded in killing his gunner 12793 Air Mechanic 1. F.Suthurst.

38.

Altun Kopri was again bombed on the 20th by four R.E.8's of No.30 Squadron escorted by a Bristol Monoplane of No.72 Squadron. This raid was in retaliation for the bombing by E.A. of Kirkuk on the 18th. Thirty 20 lb. bombs, were dropped and twelve O.K's obtained on camps and horse lines, causing severe casualties to personnel and horses. Machines came under heavy and accurate A.A. fire but all returned safely. Two enemy machines were prevented from leaving the aerodrome by Lieutenant Thomas in the Bristol Monoplane, who scattered the personnel with machine gun fire.

Major J.Everidge assumed command of No.30 Squadron on the 24th vice Major Westendarr who assumed command of No.72 Squadron on this day.

Three machines of "C" Flight of No.30 Squadron moved from Tuz Khurmatli to Kifri on the 26th.

The British troops commenced to withdraw from Kirkuk on the 11th, leaving a small mobile column as garrison, which also withdrew on the 24th. At the end of the month the British advanced posts in South Kurdistan were back at Tuz Khurmatli and Kifri.

On the Euphrates front there were no active operations, a few reconnaissances only being carried out.

On the 31st the disposition of No.30 Squadron was as follows:-

Headquarters, "A" and ½ "C" Flight		Baquba
"B" Flight		Ramadi
½ "C" Flight		Kifri

June 1918.
209/25/19.
207/72.
15/229/2.

From the beginning of June flying was reduced to the minimum on account of the heat. On the 4th a reconnaissance to Altun Kopri by three R.E.8's escorted by a Bristol Monoplane revealed no change. One A.E.G. and four Scouts were observered on the Kifri aerodrome. Three of the Scouts took off and followed the formation half way to Altun Kopri but did not attempt to engage. Sulaimaniya was reconnoitred by one R.E.8 on the 14th but nothing of import observed. On the 19th 79 plates were exposed over the Taza-Tauq area for the purpose of map compilation.

On the 26th four machines carried out two reconnaissances and demonstrations over the Sermil area where tribes in the vicinity had been giving trouble. The sight of aeroplanes appears to have had a powerful deterrent effect on the unruly element, who submitted to all the Political officers' terms rendering ground action by the punitive expedition of the 14th Division unnecessary.

On the Euphrates front flying was mostly confined to test and practice flights. One or two reconnaissances of the Khan Baghdadi-Haditha area were made.

A small column left Sahiliya on the 22nd with the object of rounding up some Turks at Khan Baghdadi. One officer and sixteen men were captured on the 23rd. Two R.E.8's from Ramadi co-operated with this column.

207/72.
d/18/31.8.18.

Experiments with carrier pigeons were carried out on the 23rd and 30th. On the first occasion two pigeons were released at 5000 feet over Wadi Huran (60 miles from Ramadi). One pigeon returned to Ramadi in 2 hrs. 20 mins. and the other in 3 hrs. 23 mins. On the 30th the same pigeons were thrown from a machine over Haditha. The times taken to reach Ramadi (about 80 miles) were 1 hr. 50 mins. and 2 hrs. 3 mins.

July, 1918.

During the first week of July "A" Flight from Baquba relieved "C" Flight at Kifri.

209/25/20.
207/72.
15/229/2.

A bombing raid was carried out on the 8th by two machines against hostile Kurds who had been holding up a military patrol at the Kargamil Pass. Sixteen 20 lb. bombs were dropped on tribal camps, sheep and cattle. 11 O.K's were obtained. 800 rounds of S.A.A. were fired into the camps from 100 feet with good effect.

On the 9th a photographic reconnaissance was carried out over the Taza Khurmatli and Tauq Chai areas. 162 plates were exposed during this reconnaissance which lasted 3 hrs. 40 mins.

An inspection of the Tuz Khurmatli defences was made by the Brigade Major of the 40th Infantry Brigade in an R.E.8 piloted by Lieutenant A.D.S.Catling.

On the 20th Major-General L.C.Dunsterville, C.B. was flown from Baghdad to Qasr-i-Shirin by Major J.Everidge.

There was practically no flying done on the Euphrates front during the month. A reconnaissance to Haditha was done on the 14th, no movement or change was reported. On the 30th one R.E.8 was sent to Rahaba to co-operate with Colonel G.E. Leachman, C.I.E., against hostile Arabs on the Lower Euphrates. The machine was not used owing to negotiations with another tribe resulting in the temporary suspension of operations.

August 1918.
209/25/21.
207/72.

During the early morning of the 3rd two E.A. attempted to approach Kifri, but were chased back to Kirkuk by three R.E.8's of No.32 Squadron and two Bristol Monoplanes of No.72 Squadron. A reconnaissance was carried out during the patrol but no enemy troops were seen at Kirkuk, Taza Khurmatli or Tauq.

Major Everidge with Captain Anderson (Acting Political Officer) as passenger in an R.E.8, using Surmil as a temporary base, carried out a low flying reconnaissance and demonstration over Gavarreh, Taktgar Bibian and Khubiar on the 8th, where turbulent tribes were inclined to be hostile to a friendly Shaikh. This had the necessary restraining effect.

Captain L.M.S.Page and Lieutenant L.Kirwan were killed in an accident at Baquba on the morning of the 20th whilst engaged on machine-gun practice. The machine stalled at a height of about 600 feet and spun into the ground. Captain Page was the senior Flight Commander and had been with "C" Flight since 1916. Lieutenant Kirwan was the most recent officer to join the squadron as an observer.

Information was received from the 14th Division on the evening of the 21st that the enemy were preparing to rush our post at Maidan. A reconnaissance ordered by G.H.Q. was carried out on the 22nd by an R.E.8 escorted by two machines. Tents were seen at Halabja but no guns observed. About 30 men believed to be Turks from their formation were seen two miles along road north-east of Halabja. The area on the left bank of the Diyala within ten miles of Maidan was searched from 1,500 feet, no signs of any hostile parties were seen. One machine landed at Mirjana and a report made to the 14th Division. Subsequent information received reported that the Maidan post was rushed by some 500 Kurds under a Turkish Officer before dawn on this day.

Captain G.Cory-Wright of "B" Flight in an R.E.8 with the object of co-operating in a special mission, flew from Rahaba with the intention of landing at Bir Shebeika, some 75 miles distant. Colonel Leachman had proceeded with an advance party to discover a good landing ground. Captain Cory-Wright searched for four hours but failed to locate Colonel Leachman. The pilot therefore returned to Rahaba.

September, 1918.
209/25/22.
209/25/25.
207/72.

During September the following moves took place:-

Three machines of "A" Flight made a non-stop flight from Kifri to Hamadan on the 17th, a distance of 200 miles over mountainous country to reinforce a detachment of No.72 Squadron working in Persia. Three days after arrival two machines were detached at Zinjan.

"B" Flight at Ramadi was relieved by a half flight of No.63 Squadron on the 17th and joined the half-flight of "A" Flight at Kifri on the 18th.

On the Diyala front reconnaissances were made of the Maidan-Halebja area on the 1st, 2nd and 27th. No movements or signs of the enemy were observed. Several practice shoots with the artillery were carried out. On the Euphrates front a reconnaissance of the Wadi Huran area revealed no change of importance. No E.A. were encountered on these fronts during the month.

The deatched half-flight in Persia working from the aerodrome at Zinjan reconnoitred roads in the vicinity of Mianeh, Turcomanchi and Ardebil and on the 25th dropped propaganda on the Palestine operations in these areas.

It was found in Persia that owing to the thinness of the air, some difficulty was experienced in getting R.E.8's in the air. Flying speed was only attained after a run of 450 yards.

October 1918.
209/253.
207/72.
21/6/87.
15/229/2.

On the 5th October orders were issued to Lieutenant-General Sir W.R.Marshall, K.C.B., to commence offensive operations against the Turkish Sixth Army which was covering the approaches to Mosul on the Tigris. The main operations on the Tigris were entrusted to Lieutenant-General Sir A.S. Cobbe, V.C., Commanding the I Corps. To protect the right flank of General Cobbe's advance, a small column from the III Corps under the command of Brigadier-General A.C.Lewin, C.B., was detailed to advance on the line Tauq-Taza Khurmatli-Kirkuk-Altun Kopri with a view to preventing the Turkish forces in that area moving down the Little Zab to reinforce the Fat-Ha position.

No.63 Squadron (less half a flight at Ramadi) and "A" Flight of No.72 Squadron at Samarra were detailed to co-operate with the I Corps on the Tigris front and No.30 Squadron at Baquba and Kifri (less half a flight in Persia) and "C" Flight of No.72 Squadron at Mirjana were attached to General Lewin's column on the Diyala front.

Prior to the main attack which opened on the 23rd No.30 Squadron kept the areas from Tuz Khurmatli as far as Halebja on the Diyala and to Kirkuk under general observation. The roads Tuz Khurmatli-Tauq-Taza Khurmatli-Kirkuk were constantly patrolled and all movements and dispositions of the enemy reported to Lewin's column.

On the 18th Lieutenant F.S. Maxwell, observer Lieutenant R.J. McNab whilst on patrol with the column observed small groups of enemy cavalry on the Tauq-Taza Khurmatli road. These were machine-gunned with good effect. Enemy camps at Taza Khurmatli were found intact and were machine-gunned at 6.30 a.m. At 7.45 Lieutenant Adams, observer Captain A.H. Mellows found all camps struck and the enemy retreating along the Kirkuk road. These were immediately attacked and information concerning the retreat dropped on the cavalry and column Headquarters. Tauq was occupied by Lewin's column on this day.

Major Everidge and Lieutenant Adams in R.E.8's bombed Kirkuk aerodrome with twelve 20 lb. bombs on the 19th. Slight damage was done to an E.A. on the aerodrome and an O.K. scored on tents. This was in retaliation for a raid made by an E.A. on Ain Nukhaila the previous day in which several casualties occurred among British and Indian O.Ranks.

On the morning of the 23rd General Lewin's column advancing from Tauq occupied Taza Khurmatli without opposition. Major Everidge, observer Lieutenant A. Bentley carried out a reconnaissance of Altun Kopri from Kifri. A message was dropped on column headquarters detailing the general position. On the return journey enemy troops holding a position south of Kirkuk with four guns and some 250 men was attacked with machine-gun fire, causing severe casualties. Later during the morning three machines, led by Major Everidge bombed and machine-gunned camps and troops in the vicinity.

On the 24th the advance on Kirkuk was continued, but some opposition was encountered at Taziyan, a village two miles south-west of Kirkuk, which was held by infantry supported by two field batteries. Lieutenant Adams, observer Captain Mellows, ranged a battery of the 66th Bridage R.F.A. on to 75 Turks in a nullah south of the village. Seven rounds were observed and one O.K. obtained; attention was then turned to a hostile gun in action to the west of the village; eleven rounds had been ranged when the gun pulled out and retreated towards Kirkuk. Three contact patrols with the column were carried out during the course of which guns, troops and transport retreating towards Kirkuk were heavily machine-gunned. Information as to all enemy movements were dropped on column headquarters. Lieutenant Adams dropped eight 20 lb. bombs from 1,000 - 2,000 feet on an enemy battery and troops. One O.K. was obtained and the remaining bombs fell within ten yards of their objective. Lieutenants E.M. Jenoure and F.S. Maxwell in R.E.8's bombed and machine-gunned shelters and E.A. on Altun Kopri aerodrome, dropping six 20 lb. bombs and firing 400 rounds of S.A.A.

An advanced landing ground was established at Brigade Headquarters six miles south of Kirkuk on the 25th for the purpose of carrying out contact and artillery patrols. On this day Lieutenants Maxwell and McNab landed on Kirkuk aerodrome prior to the departure of the enemy and were greeted by a hot fire. They were fortunate enough to get off again although the machine was considerably "shot about".

Whilst escorting a reconnaissance over the Kirkuk area Lieutenant S.D. Macdonald of "C" Flight No.72 Squadron forced landed six miles from Altun Kopri. Lieutenant Adams in an R.E.8 landed beside him, helped to burn the machine and flew him back to Tuz Khurmatli. In the meantime other machines of "C" Flight circled above in the vicinity to keep off a small group of enemy cavalry that were in the neighbourhood.

The bombing and machine-gunning of the retreating troops was continued and by 5.30 p.m. the enemy had been driven from Taziyan and had commenced to withdraw from Kirkuk. At dusk our patrols entered Kirkuk and by 3.0 a.m. on the 26th the town was entirely in our hands. Possession was taken of the aerodrome early in the morning, a dump of petrol, oil and stores established and three machines of No.30 Squadron stationed there.

A reconnaissance carried out at 7.0 a.m. on the 26th reported that all positions and gun pits north of Kirkuk had been evacuated. No movement was seen on the Kirkuk-Yarvali road, and the Yarvali - Altun Kopri road was carefully searched to about 15 miles north of Yarvali but no movement of any sort was seen.

General Lewin's column advanced on this day towards Altun Kopri, his cavalry and armoured cars encountering the enemy's rear guard some ten miles from that place. Later the further progress of the column was blocked by a river which was impassable for the armoured cars, and the column bivouacked seventeen miles north of Kirkuk. Owing to supply difficulties, further operations by Lewin's column had, after this, to be limited to action by the cavalry and armoured cars and guns. These operations carried out during the next few days harassed and contained the enemy who was holding a bridgehead at Altun Kopri.

On the 27th Captain G.Cory-Wright with Lieutenant S.P.J.Yeats as observer, escorted by two Bristol monoplanes of No.72 Squadron, carried out a reconnaissance of the Altun-Kopri-Erbil area. A small trench system at Erbil and movements of cavalry, etc. were reported upon and ten 20 lb. bombs dropped on camps and aerodrome at Altun Kopri. Two O.K's. were obtained on tents and one bomb fell between two aeroplanes which were fifteen yards apart.

Enemy resistance around Altun Kopri stiffened appreciably on the 28th. Lieutenant Adams in an R E.8., escorted by a Bristol Monoplane, attacked camps and troops with bombs and machine-gun. Eight 20 lb. bombs were dropped out of which six O.K's. were obtained; 700 rounds of S.A.A. were fired. Several tents were destroyed and many men and horses killed and wounded.

Reconnaissances of Altun Kopri were again carried out on the 29th and 30th.

During the morning of the 30th Ismail Hakki Bey commanding the Turkish troops on the Tigris surrendered with his entire force; this naturally reacted upon the Altun Kopri situation and during the night the enemy evacuated their position and retreated towards Mosul. Altun Kopri was occupied without opposition on the morning on the 31st. Armistice was signed between the British and Turkish Governments on that day.

At the end of October Headquarters "B" and "C" Flights and half of "A" Flight were stationed at Kifri.

209/25/31.
207/72.
15/229/2.
209/25/23.

The work of the detached half flight at Zinjan in Persia during October consisted mostly of reconnaissance work in the Mianeh-Jamalabad-Tabriz-Sain Kala areas. Bombs were carried and dropped on suitable targets.

On the 11th three R.E.8's of No.30 Squadron led by Captain Nuttall and escorted by two Martinsydes of No.72 Squadron reconnoitred the Mianeh-Karabana-Basmij area. A good deal of transport was observed moving towards Tabriz. New trenches were being dug on the Shibli Pass. In conjunction with this reconnaissance an offensive ground patrol and bomb raid was undertaken. Eighteen 20 lb. bombs were dropped on and 1250 rounds of S.A.A. fired at transport and troops on the Tabriz road between the Shibli Pass and Turcomanchi. Considerable damage was done and casualties estimated at about 100 men and animals were inflicted.

During the raid Lieutenant K.M.Pennington of No.72 Squadron was shot down from the ground but landed safely forty miles behind the enemy's lines. Lieutenants A.E.Morgan and J.Chacksfield of No.30 Squadron in an R.E.8 landed and picked him up. Unfortunately, however, the R.E.8 crashed on taking off and the three officers were compelled to make for the hills, machines in the air kept off hostile troops in the vicinity. After many vicissitudes these officers regained our lines at Akhmazar on the 18th after covering a distance of 120 miles over difficult and mountainous country.

A successful contact patrol with L.A.M.B. Cars and cavalry over Jamalabad to Qaplan Kuh was carried out on the 14th by Lieutenants A.H.Anson and J.B.Case in an R.E.8. A party of troops was vigorously machine-gunned. This was repeated by Lieutenants Phillips and T.A. Tindle on the 19th.

Captain Nuttall with Lieutenant Tindle carried out a reconnaissance of the Mianeh-Jamalabad district on the 24th. Camps, movements and strength of the enemy were reported upon. Four 20 lb. bombs were dropped on a camp near Mianeh and 650 rounds of S.A.A. fired at scattered troops and cavalry on roads.

Lieutenant A.E.Morgan with Captain J.Durward, Wing Headquarters photographic officer, carried out a photographic reconnaissance of the Mianeh-Jamalabad area on the 30th; the town of Kasvin was also photographed by Lieutenant Phillips and Captain Durward.

November 1918.
209/25/32.
207/72.
15/229/2.

During the period 10/23rd Headquarters and "C" Flight of No.30 Squadron moved from Kifri to Baquba and between 24/30th "B" Flight moved from Kifri to Baghdad.

Flying was mainly confined to photographic tests and artillery co-operation practice.

Major Everidge with Lieutenant F.C. de L.Kirk carried out a contact patrol on the 30th with the 37th Brigade. After the practice Major Everidge delivered a lecture on contact patrol work to the 14th Divisional Platoon School.

"A" Flight in Persia moved from Zinjan to Kasvin on the 13th and took over three Martinsyde Scouts from No.72 Squadron who were returning to Baghdad. The work during the month was mainly photographic.

On the 15th Lieutenant A.L.G.Campbell, with Captain Durward as passenger, flew from Kasvin to Hamadan and completed the photographing of the latter place on the 17th. On the 20th they completed the photographic programme of Kirmanshah.

December 1918
209/25/33.
207/72.

The Civil Commissioner, Lieutenant-Colonel A.T.Wilson, was on the 1st December flown by Captain Adams on a political tour to Sulaimani, Kirkuk and thence to Baghdad and on the 11th to Hilla, Nejef and Kerbela by Captain Morgan.

Major-General W.G.H.Salmond, D.S.O., G.O.C., R.A.F., Middle East, visited by air and inspected all units with the exception of the detachment in Persia on the 2nd and 3rd.

Lieutenant R.Beresford of "A" Flight, Kasvin was reported missing on the 12th. He was last seen flying over Hamadan. Exhaustive searches were made by other machines of the flight, but it was not until the 16th that he was picked up at Kherlieh some forty miles from Hamadan, suffering from fever.

The towns of Resht and Enzeli were photographed by "A" Flight during the 8/14th.

On the 28th Lieutenants S.Bull and C.Brears left Baquba for Ahwaz and Bushire to make arrangements for the arrival of "C" Flight who were proceeding there for the forthcoming operations against the Qashqai Tribe, who had been giving trouble in the country surrounding Shiraz and the Bushire-Kazarun-Shiraz road. This tribe seemed not unlike the tribes on the N.W. Frontier of India in their manner of raiding and fighting in the hills. The ground forces seldom got into touch with them, consequently aeroplanes played an important part in their subjugation.

January 1919.
209/25/34.

On the 1st January the personnel and transport of "C" Flight left Baquba by rail and road for Baghdad and proceeded thence to Bushire by river boat and steamer arriving on the 13th.

On the 7th two R.E.8's left Baghdad en route for Bushire, one of which carried Lieutenant-Colonel A.T.Wilson, the Civil Commissioner, as passenger, arriving on the 9th. A third R.E.8 arrived on the 10th. Major Everidge in an R.E.8, accompanied by two others, left Baghdad on the 14th. Major Everidge arrived at Bushire on the 16th, followed by the other two machines on the 17th.

Captain Adams and Lieutenant A.W.Hawkins bombed the rebel tribes' headquarters at Talheh on the 10th. Twelve 20 lb. bombs were dropped, all of which were O.K's, on the village and sheep. On the 27th four R.E.8's led by Captain Adams dropped thirty-two 20 lb. bombs on Robatak; many O.K's were observed on huts and houses. This raid was repeated on the following day by a formation of five machines led by Major Everidge. The tents had disappeared and the inhabitants ran out and took cover in nullahs on the appearance of the aeroplanes, nevertheless thirty-six 20 lb. bombs were dropped with good results on houses and also on a convoy of camels and donkeys. Twenty-five O.K's were obtained.

During this period several reconnaissances were made of the Kazarun area and of villages in the direction of the Mund river.

On the 28th the Bushire column occupied Kazarun and on the same day a column from Shiraz reached Mian Kutal.

A landing ground was established at Bandar Dilam and another on the coast at Daiyar on the 31st. The latter place could be supplied with petrol and oil, etc. by sea transport. A further landing ground was in course of preparation at Shiraz.

Owing to bad weather little flying was done by the flight at Kasvin during the month. Mails were flown to and dropped on Zinjan on the 17th and 28th, all other means of communication having been interrupted by the weather.

"B" Flight at Baghdad made several flights during the month ferrying Political officers to different parts of the country and also carrying despatches to isolated units.

Captain Nuttall in an R.E.8 with Major V.Buxton SOII (Air) Wing Headquarters as observer, and Captain Morgan with Lieutenant Baddiley of No.72 Squadron as observer, accompanied by Major O.T.Boyd, the Wing Commander on a Bristol Monoplane, carried out a bomb raid on hostile arabs of the Albu Janash Section in the Samawa area on the 31st. Sixteen 20 lb. bombs were dropped and 1237 rounds of S.A.A. fired, resulting in five people being killed and nine wounded. A few houses were smashed, cattle and sheep killed and other damage caused.

February 1919.
209/25/35.
207/72.

On the 18th February "A" Flight at Kasvin was transferred to No.63 Squadron.

The work of "B" Flight at Baghdad consisted in ferrying Political officers on urgent duty, carrying despatches and photographic work.

On the 12th Lieutenant G.V. de Boissiere flew three lakhs of rupees about £20,000 to Mosul for the Treasury Officer as all roads were impassable.

On the 14th Captain Morgan, observer Lieutenant Baddiley in an R.E.8 accompanied by Lieutenant Pope of No.63 Squadron with Major V.Buxton as observer carried out a bomb raid against hostile arabs near Nasiriya. Twelve 20 lb. bombs were dropped and seven O.K's obtained. Several casualties were caused but the machines were badly shot about by rifle fire from the ground. Major Buxton was wounded in the face.

On the 19th a machine left Bushire for Kaki carrying messages from the Consul General to the Governor of Kaki. On arrival the machine was heavily fired upon from the village. On the following day Captain Adams in a Martinsyde Scout with three R.E.8's dropped thirty-one 20 lb. bombs on and fired over 1000 rounds of S.A.A. into the village. Twenty-three O.K's were obtained causing considerable damage to houses and cattle. On this occasion the machines did not meet with rifle fire.

209/25/36.

Several reconnaissances were carried out from Bushire in March. During the late afternoon of the 6th Captain Adams, who was participating in a bomb raid over Khun, was seen to crash badly whilst machine-gunning from a low altitude. This officer's body was eventually recovered and brought into our lines when it was discovered that he had been shot through the head by rifle fire.

Operations from Bushire were now practically finished and No. 30 Squadron began to reduce to cadre. By the 2nd April the detachment at Bushire had been reduced to two machines, two pilots and 11 O.Ranks; by the 9th the reduction was complete and the cadre stationed at Baghdad.

Copy extract from AH.209/24/17.

Report of Wing Commander R.Gordon, D.S.O., R.N.A.S. on Food Carrying by Aeroplanes and Seaplanes, 15th to 29th April, 1916.

The machines available for this duty were 4 Betucis, 1 H.F. Voisin, 1 Voisin, and 3 Short Sunbeam seaplanes. These seaplanes were unfortunately not very successful as they were out of shape owing to the heavy gale in the beginning of April, and also to the fact that they were unable on many occasions to get off the water from various causes.

The majority of the food was dropped from the land machines, but the seaplanes carried a certain amount.

I. Average weight carried by each class of machine.

1. Betuci.   150 lbs. distributed in 3 loads.
2. H.F. Voisin.   200 lbs. in one load.
3. Voisin.   150 lbs. in one load.
4. Seaplanes.   200 to 250 lbs. in one load.

II. Method of attaching and releasing loads.

The best method for the land machines was found after trial of several methods and was invented by Captain Murray, R.F.C. I ordered all machines to be fitted with this device.

It consisted of a long bar attached to a bomb frame, from which the bomb guides and fittings were stripped. This bar was pivoted at one end and the other end made fast by means of a quick release which could be released from the pilot's seat.

The tops of two 50 lb. bags were then sewn together and the bags hung down on each side of the bar. When the rod was released the bags slid off. On no occasion did this hang up.

The Betucis in order to distribute the weight as much as possible on an inherently stable machine, carried two 25 lb. bags in this way slung just below the fuselage between the chassis struts, and also a 50 lb. bag on each wing close up against the fuselage. This was fastened by a slip knot and the pilot pulled the bag over the trailing edge of the wings when he wished to release the bags. This also worked very successfully.

The seaplanes were unable to carry the bags on this bar as the bags hung down into the water. They had a broad canvas band strapped under the bomb frame released by a quick release device from the pilot's seat. This was put tightly round the bags, and hung up on one occasion. The Voisin and H.F. Voisin carried the entire load slung on the bar without difficulty.

III. Height from which loads were dropped.

All food dropping was done by day. The heights were all from 5,000 to 7,000 feet. No lower was possible because as soon as the Turks became aware of what was going on they made every effort to stop it by gun fire. From a statement made by a Turkish prisoner a lot of extra enemy guns were moved round Kut to try and shoot the machines down. It was of common occurrence for a machine to come back with holes in the planes but no record of the number of machines hit was kept.

IV.

All food was dropped in ordinary S.& T. sacks. These were double one insude the other.* At first I considered that sacks were dangerous for Pusher type of machines to carry and tins were used for these two machines, but tins were abandoned owing to the damage and loss of food food when these dropped.

V.

The Kut garrison reported that the food dropped in sacks was received undamaged. The sacks appeared to spread out in the air and did not attain any great velocity.

VI.

A great number of medical dressings and drugs were dropped was well as large sums of money including 10,000 lira in wooden boxes. The money was packed very tight in these boxes without any packing and the boxes buried themselves on impact and I understand that very little was lost. A small amount of food was dropped into the Turkish lines or in the river. This was owing to the curious trajectory often assumed by the bags, which lost their forward speed at once and seem to have been blown about by the wind.

The effect of fastening the bags on the inherently stable Betuci was most marked, making the machine extremely difficult to fly. The head resistance was very great and out of all proportion to the weight. I consider that the absence of accidents was most praiseworthy and only very skilled pilots could have carried out these flights in all weathers, so successfully.

The total amount of food carried was just over 19,000 lbs. but the amount of money, dressings, etc., added largely to this total weight.

The best machine for the purpose was undoubtedly the H.F. Voisin which put by far the largest amount of food into the town.

(Signed). R. Gordon,

Wing Commander.

---

* The inner sack being tight and the outer a loose covering.

Notes on report re supply of food by
aeroplane to Kut al Amarah.
April 1916.

(a) The first load of food was dropped on 11th April, 1916. The organised daily dropping commenced on 15th April and continued to 29th April.

(b) It is understood that 5,000 lira were dropped, not 10,000.

(c) Over 19,000 pounds of food were taken.

Kut al Amarah acknowledged the receipt of approximately 16,800 pounds.

No. 30 Squadron.

Flying Casualties.

Rank.	Name.	Date.	Type of Casualty.
Lieutenant.	G.P.Merz, A.F.C.	30. 7.1915.	K. in A.
Lieutenant.	W.A.W.Burn, N.Z.A.C.	"	K. in A.
Lieutenant.	W.H.Treloar, A.F.C.	16. 9.1915.	P. of W.
Captain.	B.S.Atkins.	"	P. of W.
Captain.	T.W.White, A.F.C.	13.11.1915.	P. of W.
Captain.	F.C.C.Yeats-Brown.	"	P. of W.
Major.	H.L.Reilly.	20.11.1915.	P. of W.
Lieutenant.	E.J.Fulton.	22.11.1915.	P. of W.
Lieutenant.	R.H.Peck.	5. 3.1916.	K. in A.
Captain.	W.G.Palmer.	"	K. in A.
Captain.	J.W.Thomson-Glover.	7. 4.1916.	Injured accidentally.
Lieutenant.	D.A.L.Davidson.	26. 4.1916.	W. in A.
Captain.	S.C.Winfield-Smith.	29. 4.1916.	P. of W.
Captain.	T.R.Wells.	"	P. of W.
Captain.	R.D.Corbett.	"	P. of W.
Captain.	S.C.B.Mundy.	"	P. of W.
Lieutenant.	C.H.C. Munro.	"	P. of W.
Lieutenant.	Hon. J.H.B.Rodney.	13. 8.1916.	W. in A.
Captain.	L. King-Harman.	26.10.1916.	Killed accidentally.
Lieutenant.	T. Haywood.	"	Killed accidentally.
Lieutenant.	A.R.Rattray.	24. 2.1917.	W. in A.
Captain.	C.O.Pickering.	15. 4.1917.	K. in A.
Second-Lieutenant.	H.W.Craig.	"	K. in A.
Lieutenant.	M.L.Maguire.	28. 4.1917.	P. of W. Wounded.
Lieutenant.	J.E.Lander.	6. 5.1917.	P. of W. Wounded.
Captain.	G.Merton.	28. 9.1917.	W. in A.
Lieutenant.	A.N.Leeson.	22.10.1917.	Killed accidentally.
Lieutenant.	J.B.Welman.	31.10.1917.	P. of W. Wounded.
Second-Lieutenant.	W.Taylor.	17. 1.1918.	P. of W.
Lieutenant.	A.S.Mills.	"	P. of W.
Second-Lieutenant.	W.S.Bean.	21. 1.1918.	K. in A.
P/11439 Lance-Sergeant.	R.G.Castor.	21. 1.1918.	K. in A.
Captain.	L.W.Haight.	4. 3.1918.	P. of W.
Lieutenant.	H.L.W.Hancock.	"	P. of W.
Second-Lieutenant.	E.C.Kinghorn.	10. 3.1918.	W. in A.
Captain.	F.C.Nuttall.	27. 4.1918.	W. in A.
Lieutenant.	J.O.Allison.	15. 5.1918.	K. in A.
Lieutenant.	F.W. Atherton.	"	K. in A.
12793 Air Mechanic I.	F.Suthurts.	15. 5.1918.	K. in A.
Captain.	L.M.S. Page.	20. 8.1918.	Killed accidentally.
Lieutenant.	L.Kirwan.	"	"
Captain.	A.P.Adams.	6. 3.1919.	K. in A.

Killed in Action.	12
Wounded in Action.	6
Prisoners of War.	18
Killed accidentally.	5
Injured accidentally.	1
	42

1916.

	Pilots.		Machines.	Machines.		
	A.	N.A.	Types.	S.	U.	N.E.
W.E. 22. 7.16.	17	1	B.E.2c. Steel Henri Farman Maurice Farman Voisins	12 3 2	8 1 4 1	
W.E. 29. 7.16.	17	1	B.E.2.c. Steel Henri Farman Maurice Farman Voisins	12 3 2	8 1 4 1	
W.E. 5. 8. 16.	17	1	B.E.2.c. Steel Henri Farman Maurice Farman Voisins	12 3 2	8 1 4 1	
W.E. 12. 8.16.	20	2	B.E.2.c. Steel Henri Farman Maurice Farman Voisins	13 3 2	7 1 4 1	
W.E. 19. 8.16.	16	4	B.E.2.c. Steel Henri Farman Maurice Farman Voisins	20 4 4 2	7 1 5 1	
W.E. 26. 8.16.	16	5	B.E.2.c. Steel Henri Farman Maurice Farman Voisins	20 4 4 2	7 1 5 1	
W.E. 6.10.16.	17	4	B.E.2.c. Henri Farman Maurice Farman Voisin Martinsyde	15 4 1 1 -	3 - 8 1 -	6 - - - 6
W.E. 13.10.16.	16	3	B.E.2.c. Voisin Maurice Farman Henri Farman Martinsyde	14 1 1 3 -	5 1 - 1 -	4 - - 1 6
W.E. 20.10.16.			B.E.2.c. Voisin Henri Farman Martinsyde	13 1 3 -	10 1 2 6	- - - -

	Pilots.		Machines.	Machines.		
	A.	N.A.	Types.	S.	U.	N.E.
W.E. 3.11.16.	15	4	B.E.2.c. Henri Farman Martinsyde Voisin	19 3 - -	4 1 - 1	8 1 6 -
W.E. 9.11.16.	15	3	B.E.2.c. Voisin Henri Farman Martinsyde	19 - 4 2	4 1 1 -	8 - - 4
W.E. 16.11.16.	17	1	B.E.2.c. Voisin Henri Farman Martinsyde	20 - 4 2	4 1 1 -	7 - - 4
W.E. 23.11.16.	18	-	B.E.2.c. Henri Farman Martinsyde	19 4 2	2 1 -	17 - 4
W.E. 30.11.16.	16	2	B.E.2.c. Henri Farman Martinsyde	18 2 3	4 3 -	6 - 3
W.E. 7.12.16.	17	2	B.E.2.c. Henri Farman Martinsyde	18 2 3	4 3 -	5 - 3
W.E. 14.12.16.	20	2	B.E.2.c. Henri Farman Martinsyde	19 1 4	4 4 2	4 - -
W.E. 21.12.16.	20	2	B.E.2.c. Henri Farman Martinsyde	19 2 6	4 3 -	3 - 2
W.E. 28.12.16.	18	2	B.E.2.c. Henri Farman Martinsyde	11 2 6	13 3 -	2 - 2

1917.

	Pilots.		Machines.	Machines.			
	A.	N.A.	Types.	S.	U.	N.E.	
W.E. 4. 1.17.	23	-	B.E.2.c. Henri Farman Martinsyde	12 4 6	13 1 1	1 - 1	
W.E. 11. 1.17.	21	-	B.E.2.c. Henri Farman Martinsyde	10 1 6	15 4 1	1 - 1	
W.E. 18. 1.17.	21	-	B.E.2.c. Henri Farman Martinsyde	12 1 6	13 3 -	- - 2	
W.E. 25. 1.17.	18	-	B.E.2.c. Henri Farman Martinsyde	11 2 6	13 2 -	- - -	
W.E. 5. 4.17.	20	-	B.E.2.c. & e. Martinsyde Bristol Scout Henri Farman	9 6 - -	14 2 - -	2* - 4 4*	*In transit from Egypt. *Being returned to Egypt.
W.E. 12. 4.17.	17	1	B.E.2.c. & e. Martinsyde Bristol Scout Henri Farman	9 5 1 -	13 2 - -	2* - 3 4*	*In transit from Egypt. *Being returned to Egypt.
W.E. 19. 4.17.	16	1	B.E.2.c. & e. Martinsyde Bristol Scout Henri Farman	8 6 2 -	13 1 - -	2* - 2 4*	*In transit from Egypt. *Being returned to Egypt.
W.E. 26. 4.17.	16	1	B.E.2.c. & e. Martinsyde Bristol Scout Henri Farman	9 5 2 -	12 2 - -	2* - 2 4*	*In transit from Egypt. *Being returned to Egypt.
W.E. 3. 5.17.	18	2	B.E.2.c. & e. Martinsyde Bristol Scout Henri Farman	9 3 2 -	12 4 1 -	2* - 1 4**	**To X. A.D. 4.5.17.
W.E. 10. 5.17.	17	2	B.E.2.c. & e. Martinsyde Bristol Scout	9 3 2	12 3 1	2* - -	*In transit from Egypt.

	Pilots.		Machines.	Machines.			
	A.	N.A.	Types.	S.	U.	N.E.	
W.E. 17. 5.17.	16	3	B.E.2.c. & e. Martinsyde Bristol Scout	8 4 -	13 2 3	2 2* -	*In transit from Egypt.
W.E. 24. 5.17.	13	3	B.E.2.c. & e. Martinsyde Bristol Scout	9 3 -	14 5 3	- 2 -	
W.E. 31. 5.17.	10	6	B.E.2.c. & e. Martinsydes Bristol Scouts	9 3 1	14 5 2	-- 2 2*	*In transit from Egypt.
W.E. 6. 9.17.	24	5	B.E.2.c. & e. Martinsyde Bristol Scout	6 4 -	4 - 1	- - -	
W.E. 13. 9.17.	26	2	B.E.2.c. & e. Bristol Scout Martinsyde	8 1 4	2 - -	- - -	
W.E. 20. 9.17.	25	3	B.E.2.c. & e. Bristol Scout S.P.A.D. Martinsyde	9 1 1 3	2 - 1 2	- - - -	
W.E. 27. 9.17.	26	9	B.E.2.c. & e. Bristol Scout Martinsyde S.P.A.D.	8 1 3 1	3 - 2 1	- - - -	
W.E. 4.10.17.	26	2	B.E.2.c. & e. Martinsyde Bristol Scout S.P.A.D.	8 3 1 2	2 2 - 1	- - - -	
W.E. 11.10.17.	24	4	B.E.2.c. & e. Martinsyde Bristol Scout S.P.A.D.	7 3 1 1	3 1 - 2	- - - -	
W.E. 18.10.17.	26	2	B.E.2.c. & e. R.E.8 Bristol Scout Martinsyde S.P.A.D.	7 1 1 3 1	4 - - - 2	- - - - -	

	Pilots.		Machines.	Machines.		
	A.	N.A.	Types.	S.	U.	N.E.
W.E. 25.10.17.	26	2	B.E.2.c. & e.	6	4	-
			R.E.8.	-	1	-
			Bristol Scout	1	-	-
			Martinsyde	3	-	-
			S.P.A.D.	2	1	-
W.E. 1.11.17.	23	3	B.E.2.c. & e.	4	6	-
			R.E.8.	1	-	-
			S.P.A.D.	1	2	-
			Vickers F.S.19.	-	2	-
W.E. 8.11.17.	23	3	B.E.2.c. & e.	5	2	-
			R.E.8.	1	-	-
			S.P.A.D.	2	1	-
			Martinsydes	-	2	-
W.E. 15.11.17.	20	3	B.E.2.c. & e.	6	1	-
			R.E.8.	2	-	-
			S.P.A.D.	2	1	-
			Martinsyde	1	1	-
W.E. 29.11.17.	20	4	B.E.2.c. & e.	6	1	-
			R.E.8.	6	1	-
			S.P.A.D.	3	-	-
W.E. 6.12.17.	20	5	B.E.2.c. & e.	3	4	-
			R.E.8.	7	-	-
			S.P.A.D.	3	-	-
W.E. 13.12.17.	20	4	B.E.2.c. & e.	5	1	-
			R.E.8.	3	4	-
			S.P.A.D.	5	-	-
W.E. 20.12.17.	19	6	B.E.2.c. & e.	2	4	-
			R.E.8.	4	3	-
			S.P.A.D.	1	3	-
W.E. 27.12.17.	21	3	B.E.2.c. & e.	5	2	-
			R.E.8.	5	3	-
			S.P.A.D.	1	2	-
			D.H.4.	1	-	-

MACHINES, PILOTS AND OBSERVERS.

1918.

	Pilots.		Observers.		Machines	Machines		
	A.	N.A.	A.	N.A.	Types	S.	U.	N.E.
W.E. 3. 1.18.	21	3			B.E.2.c & e R.E.8. S.P.A.D. D.H.4.	4 5 2 1	1 4 - -	
W.E.10. 1.18.	20	3	9	1	B.E.2.c & e R.E.8. S.P.A.D. D.H.4.	3 3 2 1	1 6 - -	
W.E.17. 1.18.	20	3	9	3	B.E.2.c & e R.E.8. S.P.A.D. D.H.4.	4 5 2 1	- 7 - 1	
W.E.24. 1.18.	18	1	8	3	B.E.2.c & e R.E.8. S.P.A.D. D.H.4. Martinsyde	4 5 2 1 -	2 7 - - 3	
W.E.31. 1.18.	18	1	9	1	B.E.2.c & e R.E.8. S.P.A.D. Martinsyde	3 5 2 1	- 6 - 2	
W.E. 7. 2.18.	18	-	10	1	B.E.2.c & e R.E.8. S.P.A.D. Martinsyde	2 8 2 3	- 6 - -	
W.E.14. 2.18.	18	1	9	1	B.E.2.c & e R.E.8. S.P.A.D. Martinsyde	1 13 2 2	1 3 1 -	
W.E.21. 2.18.	18	1	10	1	B.E.2.e. R.E.8. S.P.A.D. Martinsyde	1 11 1 2	- 4 2 -	
W.E.28. 2.18.	18	-	10	1	B.E.2.e. R.E.8. S.P.A.D. Martinsyde	1 12 2 2	- 3 1 1	

	Pilots.		Observers.		Machines.	Machines.		
	A.	N.A.	A.	N.A.	Types.	S.	U.	N.E.
W.E. 7. 3.18.	17	-	12	1	B.E.2.e. R.E.8. S.P.A.D. Martinsyde	1 11 3 1	- 3 1 1	
W.E.14. 3.18.	20	-	10	3	B.E.2.e. R.E.8. S.P.A.D. Martinsyde	1 12 2 3	- 3 1 1	
W.E.21. 3.18.	21	-	10	3	B.E.2.e. R.E.8. S.P.A.D. Martinsyde	1 11 2 2	- 4 1 1	
W.E.28. 3.18.	22	1	12	1	B.E.2.c. R.E.8. S.P.A.D. Martinsyde	- 11 - 3	1 3 1 1	
W.E. 4. 4.18.	20	3	12	1	B.E.2.e. R.E.8. S.P.A.D. Martinsyde	1 10 - 2	- 6 1 1	
W.E.11. 4.18.	20	2	13	1	B.E.2.e. R.E.8. S.P.A.D. Martinsyde	- 13 - 2	1 5 1 1	
W.E.18. 4.18.	18	4	13	-	B.E.2.e. R.E.8. S.P.A.D.	- 12 -	1 3 1	
W.E.25. 4.18.	18	2	12	1	B.E.2.e. R.E.8. S.P.A.D.	- 14 -	1 - 1	
W.E. 2. 5.18.	18	3	12	1	B.E.2.e. R.E.8. S.P.A.D.	- 11 1	1 5 -	
W.E. 9. 5.18.	16	4	13	-	B.E.2.e. R.E.8.	- 7	1 7	
W.E.16. 5.18.	16	4	12	-	B.E.2.e. R.E.8.	- 11	1 5	

	Pilots.		Observers.		Machines.	Machines.		
	A.	N.A.	A.	N.A.	Types.	S.	U.	N.E.
W.E.23. 5.18.	16	4	11	2	B.E.2.e. R.E.8.	- 11	1 5	
W.E.30. 5.18.	17	6	9	3	B.E.2.e. R.E.8.	- 13	1 5	
W.E. 6. 6.18.	16	7	11	1	B.E.2.e. R.E.8.	- 13	1 6	
W.E.13. 6.18.	16	7	10	3	B.E.2.e. R.E.8.	- 13	1 5	
W.E.20. 6.18.	16	7	11	3	B.E.2.e. R.E.8.	- 14	1 4	
W.E.27. 6.18.	15	7	12	3	B.E.2.e. R.E.8.	- 10	1 8	
W.E. 3. 7.18.	12	10	10	4	B.E.2.e. R.E.8.	- 13	1 5	- -
W.E.11. 7.18.	15	6	11	3	R.E.8.	12	5	-
W.E.18. 7.18.	15	6	10	4	R.E.8.	7	10	-
W.E.25. 7.18.	15	6	10	4	R.E.8.	9	8	-
W.E. 1. 8.18.	15	6	11	3	B.E.2.e. R.E.8.	- 10	11 5	- -
W.E. 8. 8.18.	13	6	12	3	B.E.2.e. R.E.8.	- 10	1 6	- -
W.E.15. 8.18.	13	7	13	8	B.E.2.e. R.E.8.	- 12	1 4	- -
W.E.22. 8.18.	15	4	13	22	B.E.2.e. R.E.8.	1 11	- 5	- -
W.E.29. 8.18.	12	7	11	4	B.E.2.e. R.E.8.	1 10	- 5	- -
W.E. 5. 9.18.	15	6	11	4	B.E.2.e. R.E.8.	1 11	- 3	- -

	Pilots.		Observers.		Machines.	Machines.		
	A.	N.A.	A.	N.A.	Types.	S.	U.	N.E.
W.E.12. 9.18.	17	3	9	6	B.E.2.e. R.E.8.	1 11	- 3	- -
W.E.19. 9.18.	19	2	12	4	B.E.2.e. R.E.8.	1 11	- 3	- -
W.E.26. 9.18.					B.E.2.e. R.E.8.	1 9	- 5	- -
W.E. 3.10.18.					B.E.2.e. R.E.8.	1 10	- 4	- -
W.E.10.10.18.					B.E.2.e. R.E.8.	1 11	- 4	- -
W.E.17.10.18.					B.E.2.e. R.E.8.	1 11	- 4	- -
W.E.24.10.18.					B.E.2.e. R.E.8.	1 13	- 3	- -
W.E.31.10.18.					B.E.2.e. R.E.8.	1 10	- 6	- -
W.E. 7.11.18.					B.E.2.e. R.E.8.	1 10	- 6	- -
W.E.14.11.18.					B.E.2.e. R.E.8.	1 12	1 3	- -
W.E.30.11.18.					B.E.2.e. R.E.8.	1 11	1 4	- -
W.E.12.12.18.					B.E.2.e. R.E.8. Martinsyde	2 13 2	- 2 1	- - -
W.E.19.12.18.					B.E.2.e. R.E.8. Martinsyde	1 11 1	1 4 2	- - -
W.E.26.12.18.					B.E.2.e. R.E.8. Martinsyde	2 12 3	- 3 -	- - -

	Pilots.		Observers.		Machines.	Machines.		
	A.	N.A.	A.	N.A.	Types.	S.	U.	N.E.
W.E. 9. 1.19.					S.E.5.A. R.E.8. B.E.2.e. Martinsyde	- 14 2 3	1 3 - -	- - - -
W.E.16. 1.19.					S.E.5.A. R.E.8. B.E.2.e. Martinsyde	- 13 2 3	1 4 - -	- - - -
W.E.23. 1.19.					S.E.5.A. R.E.8. B.E.2.e. Martinsyde	- 13 2 3	1 4 - -	- - - -
W.E. 6. 2.19.					S.E.5.A. R.E.8. B.E.2.e. Martinsyde	- 14 1 3	1 1 1 -	- - - -
W.E.28. 2.19.					R.E.8. B.E.2.e. Martinsyde	7 1 1	2 1 -	- - -
W.E. 2. 4. 19.					R.E.8. B.E.2.e.	4 1	3 -	- -

Copy extract from A.H. 15/229/2.
(History of No.30 Squadron by Major J.Everidge).

SQUADRON COMMANDERS.

Major H.L. Reilly		
Major S.D. Massy, D.S.O.	20/11/15	to 30/5/16.
Captain E.M. Murray, M.C.	31/5/16	to 7/8/16.
Major J.E. Tennant, D.S.O., M.C.	8/8/16	to 11/1/17.
Major H. de Havilland, D.S.O.	11/1/17	to 21/4/18.
Major O.A. Westendarp	21/4/18	to 23/5/18.
Major J. Everidge, M.C.	23/5/18	to 2/5/19.

FLIGHT COMMANDERS.

"A" Flight from 1916 to 1919.

Captain H.A. Petre, D.S.O., M.C.
Captain J.R. McCrindle, M.C.
Captain H. de Havilland, D.S.O.
Captain L.J. Bayly.
Captain F. Nuttall, M.C., D.F.C.

"B" Flight from 1916 to 1919.

Captain E.M. Murray, M.C.
Captain H.F.A. Gordon.
Captain C.H. Elliott Smith.
Captain G. Merton, M.C.
Captain G. Cory Wright.
Captain A.E. Morgan.

"C" Flight from 1916 to 1919.

Captain G.B. Rickards, M.C.
Captain A. Graves.
Captain L. Wanless O'Gowan.
Captain J.H. Herring, M.M., D.S.O., M.C.
Captain L.S.M. Page.
Captain F.V. Devonshire.
Captain A.P. Adams, D.F.C.

Copy extract from A.H. 15/229/2.
(History of No.30 Squadron by Major J. Everidge).

ROLL OF OFFICERS FROM 1915 to 1919.

PILOTS.

(Note this Roll is not complete in every respect).

Rank. Name.	Date of Arrival.	Date of Departure.	Remarks. Awards.
Major S.D. Massy.	20/11/15	27/6/16	D.S.O. Mentioned in Despatches, Sept., 1915, also April, 1916.
Capt. J.R. McCrindle.	10/12/15	23/12/16	Mentioned in Despatches April, 1916. Awarded M.C.
Major H.A. Petre.		22/5/16	Awarded D.S.O., 3/6/16. M.C. Mentioned in Despatches, Sept., 1915 - Gen. Sir John Nixon. Mentioned in Despatches of Maj.-Gen. Townshend, C.B., D.S.O. Mentioned in Despatches April, 1916.
Major Reilly.			Prisoner of War.
Capt. T. White.			Prisoner of War (escaped).
Lieut. Mers.			Killed by Arabs.
Lieut. Treloar.			
Lieut. Burn.			Killed by Arabs.
Lieut. Scott.			
2nd Lt. D.A.L. Davidson.	10/12/15	6/5/16	Awarded M.C., 18/5/16.
2nd Lt. R.H. Peck.			Killed 5/3/16.
Capt. F.M. Murray.	20/11/15	15/8/16	Awarded M.C. 17/4/16.
Capt. B. Winfield Smith.	20/11/15		Captured in Kut.
Capt. A. Graves.	20/11/15	5/7/16	
Colonel R.A. Bradley.	5/11/15	-/3/16	Mentioned in Despatches several times. Afterwards commanded 31st Wing. C.M.G.

Rank. Name.	Date of Arrival.	Date of Departure.	Remarks. Awards.
Capt. G.B. Rickards.	20/11/15	5/6/16	Captured in Kut. Awarded M.C., 1/1/16. Mentioned in Despatches April, 1916 and July 15th. D.S.O.
Capt. L. Wanless O'Gowan.	10/12/15	30/4/16	
Lieut. H.P.S. Clogstoun.	27/12/15	16/9/16	
2nd Lt. J.B. Walmsley.	20/11/15		
Capt. T.R. Wells.			
Lieut. R.E. Cuff.	20/11/15	22/5/16	Mentioned in Despatches April, 1916.
Capt. I.D. Trueman.	20/11/15	29/5/16	
Lieut. E.J. Fulton.			Prisoner of War 20/11/15.
Capt. G. Merton.	17/4/16	17/2/18	Awarded M.C., 20/12/16. Mentioned in Despatches 11/2/17, 14/8/17 and 15/4/18. Wounded.
2nd Lt. A. Charig.	17/4/16	21/9/16	
2nd Lt. L.E. Millar.	31/5/16	15/7/16	
Lieut. C. Chabot.	11/6/16	18/1/17	
Capt. G.A. Cadogan Gowper	21/5/16	30/6/16	
Lieut. Hon. J.H.B. Rodney	21/5/16	27/10/16	Wounded.
Capt. H.J. Edgar.	11/6/16	28/8/16	
Lieut. T. Haywood.	11/6/16	1/1/18	Killed in aeroplane accident, 26/10/16.
Lieut. J.R. Burns.	24/6/16	7/9/16	Awarded M.C. Subsequently killed flying.
Lieut. J.E. Rettie.	24/6/16	23/12/16	
2nd Lt. H.C. Hopkinson.	24/6/16	23/5/17	M.C. Wounded subsequently in France.
2nd Lt. J.E. Windsor.	6/7/16	5/10/16	
2nd Lt. E.N. Holstins.	6/7/16	28/10/16	
Lieut. J.W. Swanson.	6/7/16	10/8/16	
Capt. G.J. Adeley.	6/7/16	23/5/17	Prisoner of War, 6/5/17. Awarded M.C. 13/8/16. Wounded.
Lieut. J.E. Lander.	6/7/16	12/5/17	Mentioned in Despatches, 14/8/17.
2nd Lt. R.B. Fricker.	6/7/16	2/1/17	Despatches, 14/8/17. D.S.O.
2nd Lt. F.M.C.D. Hawker.	1/8/16	21/5/16	Posted to Command Squadron on 11/1/17. Awarded D.S.O. Mentioned in Despatches, 14/8/17, 8/3/18 and 15/4/18.
Capt. J.H. Herring.	1/8/16		
Major H. de Havilland.			

Rank.	Name.	Date of Arrival.	Date of Departure.	Remarks. Awards.
2nd Lt.	J.B. Lloyd.	1/8/16	4/4/17	Brought down in aerial combat, 28/4/17.
2nd Lt.	M.L. Maguire.	2/10/16		Prisoner of War. Awarded M.C. Died of wounds in enemy's hands.
Colonel	J.E. Tennant.	1/8/16	11/1/17	Posted to command 31st Wing, R.F.C., Mesopotamia on this date. Legion of Honour – Croix de Chevalier. Mentioned in Despatches, 12/8/17. D.S.O., M.C.
Capt.	C.H. Elliot Smith.	2/10/16	14/7/17	
2nd Lt.	G.F. Lines.	2/10/16	6/12/16	
Lieut.	B.E. Berrington.	2/10/16	28/3/18	
2nd Lt.	R.T. Colley.	19/10/16	23/5/17	
Capt.	H.F.A. Gordon.	18/10/16	4/4/17	
Lieut.	C.L. Baldwin.	2/12/16	28/7/18	Subsequently killed flying.
Capt.	L.S.M. Page.	8/12/16		Killed 20/8/17. Mentioned in Despatches, 8/3/18.
Lieut.	F.J. Tanner.	8/12/16	28/7/18	
Lieut.	A.E.L. Skinner.	8/12/16	11/4/18	Mentioned in Despatches. Awarded M.C.
Lieut.	F.O. Rose.	31/12/16	13/1/19	
Lieut.	R.K. Morris.	31/12/16	11/4/18	Mentioned in Despatches, 8/3/19. Awarded M.C.
Capt.	C.O. Pickering.	31/12/16		Killed in aerial combat, 15/4/17.
Capt.	L.J. Bayly.	3/2/17	7/10/17	Mentioned in Despatches, 14/8/17. Croix de Guerre. Mentioned in Despatches, 8/3/18. Died of wounds.
2nd Lt.	J.B. Welman.	2/5/17		Wounded and prisoner of war, 31/10/17.
2nd Lt.	W. Taylor.	1/5/17		Prisoner of war, 17/1/18.
2nd Lt.	W.S. Bean.	1/5/17		Killed in action, 21/1/18.
Capt.	F. Nuttall.	1/5/17	25/3/19	Awarded M.C., 26/3/18. Awarded D.F.C., 11/2/19. Wounded.

Rank. Name.	Date of Arrival.	Date of Departure.	Remarks.	Awards.
Lieut. A.W. Hawkins.	6/7/17	13/1/18	Mentioned in Despatches.	
2nd Lt. C. Cox.	6/7/17	28/1/18	Subsequently died in India.	
2nd Lt. P.F. West.	6/7/17	9/11/17		
2nd Lt. H.L. Gardiner.	19/7/17	4/12/17		
Capt. E.G. Baxter.	16/7/17			
Capt. A.P. Adams.	6/8/17		Killed in action, 6/3/19.	Awarded D.F.C., 31/10/18.
Capt. W.L. Haight.	17/8/17		Prisoner of war, 4/3/18.	
Lieut. J.O. Allison.	17/8/17	9/1/18	Killed in action, 15/5/18.	Awarded M.C.
Lieut. C.B.M. Dale.	17/8/17			
2nd Lt. E.M. Jenoure.	17/8/17			
Lieut. A.H. Anson.	15/7/17	13/2/19	Mentioned in Despatches.	
2nd Lt. E.J. Head.	15/7/17	17/8/17		
Capt. A.E. Morgan.	6/8/17			
Capt. G.M. Smyth.	24/8/17	7/9/18	Mentioned in Despatches.	
Lieut. L.B. Browning.	7/12/17	3/7/18	G.S.O.3 31st Wing.	
Capt. G. Cory Wright.	5/2/18	17/11/18	Awarded M.C., May, 1918.	
Lieut. E.L. Pratt.	2/3/18	16/6/18	Mentioned in Despatches.	
2nd Lt. E.T. Thorpe.	2/3/18	26/3/19		
2nd Lt. F.S. Maxwell.	7/3/18			
Lieut. A.L.G. Campbell.	18/2/18	13/2/19	Invalided.	
Lieut. L.L. Loleu.	13/3/18	28/10/18	Subsequently prisoner of war.	
Lieut. A.A. Cullen.	21/3/18	12/4/18	Commanded Squadron April and May, 1918.	
Major O.A. Westendarp.	21/4/18	12/5/18	Prisoner of war. Died in enemy's hands.	
Capt. A.S. Edwards.	12/4/18			
2nd Lt. P. Phillips.	16/4/18	13/2/19		
Lieut. A.D.S. Gatling.	16/4/18	13/2/19		
Lieut. F.W. Carryer.	6/4/18			
Lieut. R.H. McIntosh.	6/5/18	10/10/18		
Lieut. G.V. De Boissiere.	6/4/18	26/3/19		
Lieut. R. Beresford.	12/8/18	22/2/19	Invalided.	
Lieut. G. Fielden.	29/8/18			
Capt. F.V. Devonshire.	29/8/18	2/11/18	Mentioned in Despatches.	
Lieut. J.W.C.L. Gordon.	14/9/18	25/3/19		Killed in India.

Rank. Name.	Date of Arrival.	Date of Departure.	Remarks. Awards.
2nd Lt. E.N. Fletcher.	23/10/18	3/4/19	Awarded D.F.C., March, 1919.
Lieut. S. Bull.	9/11/18	3/4/19	
Lieut. E.F.H. Jolly.	9/11/18	3/4/19	Awarded M.C., May, 1918. Commanded Squadron from May, 1918, to May, 1919. Mentioned in Despatches.
Major Everidge.	25/4/18	3/4/19	

OBSERVERS.

Rank. Name.	Date of Arrival.	Date of Departure.	Remarks. Awards.
Capt. W.G. Palmer.			Killed in action, 5/3/16. Mentioned in Despatches, Sept., 1915.
Capt. J.R. Yeats Brown.	15/12/15	31/8/16	Prisoner of war.
Capt. B.S. Atkins.	27/12/15	21/9/16	Prisoner of war.
Capt. R.D. Corbett.	27/12/15	31/8/16	Prisoner of war.
2nd Lt. C.H.C. Munro.	5/1/16	18/9/16	Prisoner of war.
Capt. S.C.B. Mundy.	2/1/16	21/9/16	Prisoner of war.
Capt. J.O.G. Orton.	29/2/16	28/5/16	Mentioned in Despatches, April, 1916.
Capt. J.W.T. Glover.	29/2/16	21/4/16	Mentioned in Despatches, April, 1916.
Lieut. T.M. Dickinson.	29/3/16	30/4/16	Mentioned in Despatches, April, 1916.
Capt. H.H. Bagnall.	29/3/16	31/5/16	
Lieut. C.T. Sanctuary.	17/5/16	4/12/16	Awarded M.C., 13/8/16.
2nd Lt. I. Mitchell.	17/5/16	10/1/17	See above.
2nd Lt. H.D.B. Turner.	21/3/16	17/7/16	
2nd Lt. A.G. Balbernie.	23/5/16	9/10/16	
Lieut. R.O. Skinner.	19/6/16	10/1/17	Mentioned in Despatches, 14/8/17.
2nd Lt. E.A.D. Barr.	10/6/16		Killed in aeroplane accident, 26/10/16.
2nd Lt. H.L. Browning.			
Lieut. J.H.R. Giles.			
Lieut. R.F.J. Cochrane.			
Lieut. W.A. Forsyth.			
Capt. L. King Harman.			
2nd Lt. C.W.B. Norman.	24/6/16	7/10/16	On being posted to Balloon Section. Meteorological Officer.

Rank.	Name.	Date of Arrival.	Date of Departure.	Remarks. Awards.
Capt.	W.A. Hanney.		4/4/17	Recording Officer. Qualified later as observer. Relinquished appointment as R.O., 2/1/17.
Lieut.	E.A. Cresswell.	29/7/16	6/3/17	
Lieut.	L. Beever Potts.	17/8/16	4/4/17	M.C.
Capt.	F.W. Hudson.	18/8/16	4/12/16	
Lieut.	H. Richardson.	28/8/16	26/3/17	
Lieut.	St.Clair Smallwood.	29/8/16	10/1/17	
Lieut.	R.M.C. Macfarlane.	19/9/16	4/4/17	Mentioned in Despatches, 14/8/17.
Lieut.	J.A. Ainscow.	17/10/16	26/5/17	Wounded.
Lieut.	M.R. D'Arcy.	3/11/16	1/1/18	
Lieut.	A.R. Rattray.	7/11/16	4/6/17	Mentioned in Despatches, 14/8/17.
Lieut.	D. Kingsley.	25/11/16	14/8/17	
2nd Lt.	R.A.C. Beckett.	30/11/16	14/8/17	
2nd Lt.	A.E.A. Dunstan.	30/11/16	21/11/17	
Lieut.	R.A. Heron.	4/12/16	19/4/17	
Capt.	P.W. Brodie.	9/1/17	26/5/17	
Capt.	W.H. O'Neill.	4/2/17	18/6/17	M.C. Wing Adjutant.
2nd Lt.	H.W. Craig.	28/1/17	18/6/17	Killed in aerial combat, 15/4/17.
Capt. (Maj.)	A. Buxton.	14/2/17	14/10/17	Mentioned in Despatches, 8/3/18, G.S.O.2, 31st Wing. Wounded. O.B.E.
Lieut.	K.W. Mackichan.	7/4/17	4/12/17	
Lieut.	F.G.O. Dickinson.	27/4/17	23/1/18	
Capt.	L.N. Schneider.	25/4/17	23/1/18	
2nd Lt.	R.J. Eccles.	26/5/17	21/1/18	
Lieut.	A.N. Leeson.	17/1/17		Killed in action, 22/10/17. Awarded D.S.O.
Lieut.	R.R.B. Sievier.	17/1/17	21/5/18	Awarded M.C. Mentioned in Despatches, 15/4/18. Wounded.
2nd Lt.	M. Heworth Booth.	1/8/17	10/10/17	
2nd Lt.	H.J.W. Hancock.	1/8/17		Prisoner of war, 4/3/18.

Rank. Name.	Date of Arrival.	Date of Departure.	Remarks. Awards.
2nd Lt. S.R. Stranger.	1/9/17	18/10/17	
Lieut. W.F. Creery.	25/10/17	22/5/18	Awarded bar to M.C. Mentioned in Despatches, 15/4/18.
2nd Lt. A.H.E. Lindop.	30/10/17	22/5/18	Awarded M.C.
Lieut. R.C. Williams.	1/11/17	20/6/18	
Lieut. D. Craik.	8/11/17	17/6/18	Wounded in action.
Lieut. S. Barnes.	22/11/17	20/8/18	
Lieut. A.S. Mills.	2/1/18	17/4/18	Prisoner of war, 17/1/18.
2nd Lt. C.G. Bushe.	2/1/18	26/10/18	
2nd Lt. E.G. Kinghorn.	29/1/18	4/11/18	Wounded in action.
Lieut. M.C. Atherton.	1/2/18		M.C. Killed in action, 15/3/18.
Lieut. J.B. Case.	18/2/18	4/11/18	
Lieut. R.J. McNab.	5/3/18	23/11/18	
Lieut. E.M. Neame.	5/4/18	17/4/18	
2nd Lt. H. Morden Wright.	2/3/18	20/9/18	M.C.
Lieut. F.C. Kirk.	5/3/18	1/1/19	
Capt. A.H. Mellows.	21/5/18	21/6/18	Mentioned in Despatches.
2nd Lt. M.J. O'Connell.	2/5/18	26/5/18	Subsequently killed.
2nd Lt. J.H.P. Southan.	2/6/18	12/12/18	
Lieut. V. Soper.	4/6/18	10/1/19	Invalided.
Lieut. T.A. Tindle.	11/6/18	25/12/18	
2nd Lt. S.P.J. Yeats.	15/6/18	18/12/18	
2nd Lt. A. Bentley.	15/6/18	18/12/18	
2nd Lt. C. Brears.	16/6/18	22/2/19	
Lieut. Kirwan.	1/8/18	13/2/19	
2nd Lt. J. Chacksfield.	5/8/18	28/12/18	Killed flying, 20/8/18.
Lieut. R.T. Carter.	15/9/18	18/3/19	
Lieut. C.H.H. Holland.	17/10/18	25/3/19	
Capt. E.F. Carrall.	10/11/18	14/12/18	Invalided.
Lieut. C.A. Lawrenson.	19/11/18		

Rank. Name.	Date of Arrival.	Date of Departure.	Remarks.	Awards.
EQUIPMENT OFFICERS.				
Lieut. J.A. Gibson.	17/2/16	15/11/17	Stores.	
Lieut. E.R. Moxey.	10/8/16	28/7/17	Photography. Wing P.O.	Mentioned in Despatches, 14/8/17.
Lieut. W.R. Lewis.	11/6/16	18/11/17	Wireless.	
Capt. P.L. Hunting.	25/10/16	30/7/17	Wireless.	
Lieut. R.B. Herring.	31/8/17	20/5/18	Photography.	Wing P.O.
Lieut. C.H.E. Ridpath.	17/11/17	15/12/18	Wireless.	
Lieut. W.G. Lamb.	4/1/18	25/3/19	Stores.	
Lieut. H.A. Dinnage.	3/18	6/7/18	Wireless.	
2nd Lt. S.B. Henson.	21/3/18	8/2/19	Gunnery.	
2nd Lt. D.J. Moran.	5/9/18	13/2/19	Wireless.	
2nd Lt. S.G. Bunster.	26/11/18	24/3/19	Wireless.	
RECORDING OFFICERS.				
Capt. F.A. Hannay.	26/9/16	4/1/17		
Capt. G.H.W. Dennys.	4/1/17	27/1/18		
Lieut. E.D.G. Hughes.	8/3/18			

www.ingramcontent.com/pod-product-compliance
Lightning Source LLC
Chambersburg PA
CBHW081003180426
43192CB00042B/2436